Dana White

Lerner Publications Company
Minneapolis

A&E® and **BIOGRAPHY®** are trademarks of the A&E Television Networks, registered in the United States and other countries.

Some of the people profiled in this series have also been featured in A&E's acclaimed BIOGRAPHY series, which is available on videocassette from A&E Home Video. Call 1-800-423-1212 to order.

Copyright © 2000 by Anita Larsen

This book is available in two bindings:
Library binding by Lerner Publications Company
Soft cover by First Avenue Editions
Divisions of Lerner Publishing Group
241 First Avenue North
Minneapolis, MN 55401

Website address: www.lernerbooks.com

Library of Congress Cataloging-in-Publication Data

White, Dana.
    George Lucas / by Dana White
        p.   cm. — (A&E biography)
    Filmography: p. 122–123
        Includes bibliographical references and index.
        Summary: Traces the life of the man who became well-known for his Star Wars movies, from his childhood in California to his career in films.
    ISBN 0-8225-4975-1 (alk. paper). —
    ISBN 0-8225-9684-9 (pbk. : alk. paper)
        1. Lucas, George Juvenile literature. 2. Motion picture producers and directors—United States Biography Juvenile literature. [1. Lucas, George. 2. Motion picture producers and directors.] I.Title. II. Series.
PN1998.3.L835W55 2000
791.43'0233,092-dc21   99–14169

Manufactured in the United States of America
1 2 3 4 5 6 – JR – 05 04 03 02 01 00

CONTENTS

Youth Survives Crash

Just what part in saving his life the roll bar, arrow, and a safety belt played is not known, but George W. Lucas, Jr. survived this crash yesterday. The high-way patrol said the safety belt snapped and Lucas was thrown from the car, which was slammed into the tree by another vehicle in the collision.

*George's car accident appeared in the local paper. The arrow, lower left in photograph, **points to a bar that was supposed to protect George in case he rolled his tiny car.***

Chapter **ONE**

HERE FOR A REASON

IT WAS TUESDAY, JUNE 12, 1962. IN MODESTO, California, the average summer temperature is 110 degrees—hot enough to make you drowsy. But the short, skinny eighteen-year-old boy hunched over his textbooks in the downtown library wasn't put off by the heat. What bewitched George Walton Lucas Jr. was daydreams of racing cars and of the trip to Europe his dad had promised as a high school graduation gift.

Three years earlier, seeing that young George was crazy about cars, George's dad had bought him a two-cylinder Fiat Bianchina. George had been too young to get a driver's license, so he would speed down the avenues between the trees of the family's walnut ranch—small towns are often lenient on rules.

George thought the Fiat was a "dumb little car" with "a sewing machine motor," so he had souped it up at a local garage. He'd won trophies driving in area autocross races, and he'd already rolled the little car. Afterward, he removed the mashed top and installed a windscreen and roll bar, ignoring the warning to slow down.

George also ignored a harsh lesson when seven of his schoolmates died after smashing into a tree at one hundred mph. Nothing could stand in the way of the thrill of taking a corner on two wheels.

The other daydream—of his upcoming trip to Europe—wasn't a sure thing. First he had to graduate, and chances were slim that he would graduate with his class at Thomas Downey High School in just three days. A poor student, he hadn't yet written the three term papers due the next day, and he wasn't ready for final exams.

George gave up studying shortly before 5:00 P.M., grabbed his books and papers, and went outside to crawl into his Fiat. Late afternoon sun slanted through the roll bar as he set off on the familiar way home. George glanced in his rearview mirror just before he turned left onto the short dirt road leading to his house. Seeing nothing, he turned. Only then did he hear the roar of an engine and the mad honking of a car horn. Another teen's Chevy Impala was bearing down on him.

The other driver tried to swerve but couldn't. The Chevy struck the Fiat by the driver's seat. The Fiat flew sideways and flipped, again and again. On the third flip, George's seat belt snapped. Thrown clear, he landed on his chest and stomach. His car went on flipping until a walnut tree stopped it. The impact moved the tree back several feet, roots and all, leaving a huge hole in the ground. Unconscious, George bled from a gash in his forehead. He wasn't getting enough oxygen, and he was beginning to turn blue.

A neighbor heard the crash and called an ambulance. The Chevy's driver was in his car on the side of the road, dazed but unhurt. George was another matter. By the time the ambulance arrived, his heartbeat was faint and his breathing was labored. On the five-mile trip to the hospital, he coughed up bright red blood.

George didn't take his final exams the next day. The local newspaper ran a front-page story about the accident, complete with a photo of the totaled Fiat. The paper reported that George was given a ticket for making an illegal left turn. Three days later, his high school diploma was delivered to his hospital room.

Instead of traveling through Europe, George spent the summer taking trips to the hospital for physical therapy. He had a lot of time on his hands, and for the first time, he started thinking about what he wanted to do with his life.

Although Modesto, California, has grown since the days when George lived there, the city still has a midwestern feel.

Chapter **TWO**

A MIDWESTERN KIND OF UPBRINGING

GEORGE LUCAS WAS BORN AND RAISED IN MODESTO, a small farming town in California's San Joaquin Valley, just east of San Francisco. "Even though it's California, it was a quiet Midwestern kind of upbringing," George later said.

In fact, many of the townspeople were transplanted midwesterners. They brought that region's values with them—do one's duty, know right from wrong, work for what you want, strive for fairness and honesty, have faith in God. The summer after his car crash, George acquired additional certainties. He had to figure out who he was and what he wanted to do.

When George was born, on May 14, 1944, he looked a lot like his father, George Lucas Sr. The new baby

Young George, left, works with a classmate on a science project. Although George looks rather eager, he wasn't very interested in schoolwork.

boy had dark hair and eyes, a small frame—he weighed only five pounds—and had big ears that stuck out, a family trademark. No wonder he was named George Walton Lucas Jr. But his family called him Georgie when he was little to distinguish him from his father.

George Sr. ran the family business, L. M. Morris, Stationers, which sold office equipment, typewriters, toys, and paper supplies. George's mother, Dorothy, managed the household, which included George's sisters, ten-year-old Ann and eight-year-old Katherine. When little George was born, the girls waited excitedly for their mother and new brother to come home to the family's new house at 530 Ramona Avenue.

Eight months later, housekeeper Mildred Shelley—called "Till"—arrived from Missouri. She'd been hired to help Dorothy, who was frail. Till was still there three years later, when George's sister Wendy was born. A second mother to George and Wendy, Till told the kids stories, read George his favorite book, *Goldilocks and the Three Bears,* and played records for him. He liked John Philip Sousa marches best. Till was a firm, predictable, supportive anchor, and George needed that security. At six, he was still small—thirty-five pounds and three feet, seven inches tall. He was a natural target for bullies, whom his constant companion Wendy fought off. "My strongest impression was that I was always on the lookout for the evil monster that lurked around the corner," George said.

When George was six years old, he had a mystical experience. Till sometimes took him and Wendy with her on Sundays to the German Lutheran church she attended. George admired the deeply serious religious ritual. What is God, the six-year-old wondered. "More important than that, what is reality? What is this? It's as if you reach a point and suddenly you say, 'Wait a second, what is the world? What are we? What am I? How do I function in this, and what's going on here?'" George later recalled.

He gained insights from less serious sources as well. George shared toys from the shelves of his father's shop, such as water pistols and Lionel trains, with friends. He and his friends also put together backyard carnivals featuring a zoo of neighborhood pets or thrill rides made from big telephone-cable spools. The children also built *dioramas* or imaginative scenes of other worlds, complete with miniature cities and farms and houses.

George also adored comic books. He had so many that his father built a shed to house them all. Wendy and George took quilts to the shed so they could pore over the illustrated books in comfort. Through comic books, George became interested in drawing, and his teachers encouraged him. In 1949, when a friend's father bought one of the first television sets in town, George started hanging out there to watch cartoons—comic books in motion.

George Sr. waited until 1954 to buy a television. By then, the number of television sets being produced in the United States had risen, and many cities had a few channels. In Modesto, however, there was still just one channel, KRON-TV from San Francisco. Still, it gave George plenty to watch. The family's television sat on a turntable in the living room. Most nights after dinner, George and Wendy took blankets and pillows

As George grew older, he started listening to rock and roll records by singers like Chuck Berry, one of the famous rockers of the '50s and '60s.

down to the living room and turned on the television. They watched cartoons, Westerns such as *Gunsmoke*, old movies, and war stories like *Victory at Sea*. George especially loved the old black-and-white film serials like *Flash Gordon Conquers the Universe*. In the Flash Gordon shows, the hero went up against aliens—and won. Originally produced to be shown before a feature film in movie theaters, these shows had cliff-hanger endings designed to bring ticket buyers back the following week.

In a cliff-hanger ending, the hero is in trouble. His back is to the wall, and the bad guys are coming straight at him. When the next episode of the show begins, the hero suddenly spots a way out of the trouble—such as a dangling rope he can use to swing over the bad guys' heads to freedom. Of course, by the end of the episode, the hero is in a different, equally perilous situation.

When George was eleven, his family took a week-long trip to the newly opened Disneyland theme park in Anaheim, California. Lucas loved the excitement of fantasy in a spotless, safe environment.

Back home there were chores, for which the Lucas kids received weekly allowances. George's chore was to mow the lawn. Still small at eleven years old, he found it difficult to push the mower. He quietly saved his allowance for four months. When he had $35, he borrowed another $25 from his mother. Then he went out and bought a $60 power mower.

As a child, George kept to himself much of the time. Although he watched television and read comic books with his sister Wendy, she said she "never knew what he was thinking." A childhood friend said he couldn't remember much about young George: "He just didn't make that big of an impression."

George was good at blending in, getting along, and getting by during his years at Roosevelt Junior High School, even though he had trouble with reading, writing, and math. He just didn't understand why academic subjects mattered. "I would have learned how to read eventually—the same with writing," he said later. "You pick that stuff up because you have to. I think it's a waste of time to spend a lot of energy trying to beat education into somebody's head. They're never going to get it unless they want to get it."

He did, however, read "Huck Finn sorts of things," as well as his collection of Landmark books about history and geography. Many of the stories in these books told about important people who had made a difference in the world.

In 1959, George's family moved to the "ranch," a ranch-style house set among acres of walnut trees on the edge of Modesto. Out on the ranch, George became even more isolated. It was too far to bicycle into town, and neither he nor his friends had cars. To ease the transition, his father built a wood and glass case to hold the dioramas his son had built with friends before but now built mostly by himself.

George's high school senior photo doesn't show his reckless side.

George soon developed another interest. He would get home from school at 3:00 P.M., go straight to his room, and play his collection of 45 and 78 rpm rock and roll records. He sat on his bed, washing down Hershey's bars with Coca Cola, and listened to the music of singers like Elvis Presley and Chuck Berry.

George let his hair grow, greasing it with Vaseline into styles like those worn by the recording artists he admired. He didn't want his jeans washed. He put taps on his black, pointy-toed shoes. He looked like a "JD"—a juvenile delinquent—but he really didn't care about being a rebel. His major passion was cars.

By the time he entered high school, George was obsessed with cars. Even after his father gave him a 35-millimeter camera and they converted an extra bathroom into a darkroom, George took pictures of cars. Finally, his dad bought him the safest car he could find—the tiny Fiat. George was unleashed. "I had my own life once I had my car," he recalled. "Along with the sense of power and freedom came the competitiveness."

Before then, George hadn't excelled at much. With his new wheels, he was one of the fastest, craziest, bravest drivers around. He went out every night, never telling his family where. He cruised Modesto, looking for girls, fun, and drag races, hanging out with what he called "the real bad element." He piled up speeding tickets when he wasn't legally speeding for autocross trophies. Even though he'd gotten good enough at photography to sell some race pictures, he still seemed to be what his older sister Kate called him— "a total loss."

In high school, George cruised Modesto from 3:00 P.M. to 1:00 A.M. every weekday, all day on weekends. Gas was cheap, and so was stopping for a burger at the Round Table, where he could hang out with his "greaser" friends. George didn't date in high school, but he talked about girls a lot. When his near-fatal car accident totaled George's dream of a racing career along with his Fiat, his father gave him an 8-millimeter movie camera. George turned to filming cars instead of racing them. He began going out of town to see art films, independent films made for a small audience. He started reading books about film.

In the fall of 1962, after his life-changing accident, George enrolled in Modesto Junior College. He took courses in sociology, anthropology, literature, astronomy, art history, and creative writing. His grades inched up enough for him to earn his associate of arts degree on June 9, 1964.

The next step was a degree from a four-year college. A friend suggested the film school at the University of Southern California (USC), a highly ranked private school in Los Angeles. Film school would bring together many of George's interests, and since cinema studies weren't popular at the time, it would be easy to get in. George hesitated, then sent off an application. He was astonished and pleased when he was accepted into the program.

His father was also astonished—but not especially pleased. George Sr. didn't want his son living in Los Angeles, which he called "Sin City." George Jr. declared that he would never go into the family office supply business.

"Well, you'll be back in a few years," his father said.

"I'll never be back," George Jr. shouted, "and as a matter of fact, I'm going to be a millionaire before I'm thirty!"

Brave words, but first he had to get through film school.

George's father didn't think modern Los Angeles—also called the City of Angels—was any place for his son George Jr.

Chapter **THREE**

A STAR IS BORN

IN THE SUMMER OF **1964,** TWENTY-YEAR-OLD **GEORGE** moved to Los Angeles. He lived near the beach with a couple of friends, paying his share of the rent by selling paintings of surfer girls with big, sad eyes. He also looked for work. "I hit every two-bit movie company on Ventura Boulevard, a thousand of them, going from door to door. . . . I said I was looking for a job and I'd do anything. No luck."

Although his father still objected to film school, he paid his son's tuition, plus two hundred dollars a month for expenses. This, George Sr. said firmly, was a salary. School was a job that required hard work. Flunk out, you lose your job. If you need money, earn it working in the family business.

It was a reasonable deal, but George wondered if he could meet its terms. USC had the oldest and largest film school in the country. George came from a one-movie-theater town other film students had never heard of. Everybody else seemed to know what they were doing. Their heroes were great film directors like Jean-Luc Godard, Federico Fellini, and Orson Welles, or the up-and-coming director Francis Ford Coppola.

Born in 1939, Coppola was the first filmmaker of George's generation to succeed in the old Hollywood studio system. Coppola had graduated from USC's rival film school, the University of California at Los Angeles (UCLA). The film he made for his master's thesis, *You're a Big Boy Now*, was distributed by Warner Brothers as a feature film, a film that is shown in movie theaters. Coppola was living proof that success could happen.

At USC, George discovered great directors whose work he hadn't known. Classmates like director John Milius and film editor Walter Murch spurred George's exploration of the many different opportunities film had to offer. "At USC, we were a rare generation because we were open-minded," he said later. "We had guys there who did nothing but Republic serials and comic books. I was being exposed to a whole lot of movies you don't see every day. I don't know how else I could have learned so much in the time."

George made his first formal film for a class assignment. Instructor Herb Kossower told his animation class to see what they could do with a single minute's worth of film. With thirty-two feet of film, George made a one-minute piece called *Look at Life*. He leafed through several issues of *Life* magazine, shot an equal number of violent and peaceful photographs, and edited them into a dazzling, flashing sequence of images. Kossower entered the film in several film festivals, where it won awards.

"I realized that I'd found myself," George said. "I took the bit and ran with it. I was introduced to film editing . . . and I think ultimately that film editing was where my real talent was."

At the time, film editing was a hands-on production. Footage shot on celluloid film reels were run through Moviola editing machines, which showed each frame, or shot, of the film. When an editor wanted to make a cut from one scene to another, he or she would mark the scene's beginning and end with a grease pencil and literally cut out the part that was not needed. The cut film would drop onto the floor (hence the phrase "lost on the cutting-room floor"). The rest of the pieces of film were spliced together with glue to make the final film. Technological advances eventually eliminated manual film editing, but while at school, George had to do it the old-fashioned way.

George loved being a film major in a school where the emphasis was on experimenting and doing rather than on academic knowledge. He learned how to use a camera and how best to present his ideas on film.

He was becoming an artist, using film to figure out what he thought and how he could express his thoughts in a way others could understand.

The USC film department building was somewhat separated from the main campus. Film majors were in their element there, but other students thought of them as misfits. "We were looked at as a weird group of guys," George's classmate Howard Kazanjian recalled. "It was mostly guys at the time. Very few women."

As the film students developed more skills and completed more projects, they drifted into groups. Those who made exciting films became friends with others who did the same. Soon an elite clique formed. They called themselves the Dirty Dozen, a name taken from

USC's film school was so well known that the university acquired the nickname "USCinema."

a movie about some convicts turned commandos. In addition to George, the group included director Randal Kleiser, writer-director John Milius, editor Walter Murch, producer Howard Kazanjian, producer Chuck Braverman, writer-director Bob Zemeckis, director John Carpenter, and writer-director Willard Huyck. Later, along with Francis Ford Coppola and Steven Spielberg from the West Coast and filmmakers Brian De Palma and Martin Scorsese from the East Coast, the group used their friendship and mutual support to help break into the film industry.

George stood out among the Dirty Dozen. He worked even harder than his father had asked him to. He would hunch over an editing machine all night to get his films just right. When he got hungry, he would grab a candy bar or some chocolate-chip cookies and a Coke and go back into the editing booth. Celluloid film whipped through his white editing gloves, and his grease pencil marked cuts as he breathed the fumes of splicing glue.

George's work was making him a film-school star. As always, he did things his own way. Howard Kazanjian remembered George saying, "I'm gonna shoot my film in color. I'm not going to be limited to the footage I'm given or limited to the length of my completed film." He got away with it.

George's senior film, called *Freiheit*, introduced ideas that showed up again in his later work. *Freiheit* is the German word for freedom. The film deals with a

The years during the war in Vietnam were tumultuous for Americans. Many protesters gathered to burn draft cards and stage sit-ins.

student's escape from then-Communist East Germany to free West Germany, only to be shot dead. A gun-toting soldier stands over the body and says ironically, "Without freedom, we're dead." George hoped the statement would remind viewers of the war raging in Vietnam at the time. He did not agree with the U.S. policy of fighting in Vietnam as a way to protect American democracy and freedom.

On August 6, 1966, George received his bachelor of arts degree from what film majors called USCinema. But the war in Vietnam loomed like a dark shadow over everyone's future. George worried that he would be drafted into the army and plunked down with a rifle in the rice paddies of Southeast Asia. Then he learned about a more attractive possibility from some students who were in the U.S. Air Force. With his skills and training, they told George, he could become an officer in the Air Force's photography unit. Although he had previously rejected President Lyndon B. Johnson's policies in Vietnam, George decided to enlist in the Air Force and aim for officer status in the photography unit.

As it turned out, the U.S. Air Force didn't like George's plan. Because of all his teenage speeding tickets, George had a police record. He couldn't become an officer. He could still enlist, though—if he wanted to face four years of combat duty. He didn't. He thought about moving to Canada to avoid the draft, but after talking to others who had done so, he became disenchanted with that idea. Before he could come up with another plan, he was drafted.

There was nothing to do but report for the induction physical in downtown Los Angeles. The physical examination revealed that George had diabetes, a condition in which the body cannot regulate blood sugar. His grandfather had died of complications from the disease when George Lucas Sr. was only fifteen. Because of the diabetes, George Jr. could not be drafted into military service. The disease also kept him from alcohol, chocolate and other sweets, and starches.

The news that he was diabetic came as a shock to George and made him feel vulnerable. He went to see his sister Kate's husband, a physician. It was true—he was diabetic, but he had only a mild form of the disease and could be treated with medication.

By this time, it was too late for George to start work on a master's degree at USC in the fall. Once again he pounded the pavement looking for work. This time it was easier—he had samples of his work and friends in the business. He picked up jobs here and there, and then a friend recommended him to veteran film editor Verna Fields.

Fields was editing documentary films made by the United States Information Agency (USIA) to explain the United States' presence in Southeast Asia. She offered Lucas a job in early 1967. By then, George was planning to go back to graduate school and had asked his father to support him a little longer. Although his father hadn't argued, George didn't like asking for help. So he decided to postpone grad school a little longer and take the job Fields offered, as well as an assistantship to teach a special course for navy cameramen at USC. He taught by night and edited USIA films by day.

George learned from his day job that he didn't like people telling him how to edit. When the government said he couldn't show President Lyndon Johnson's bald spot, George told himself that one day he'd be an independent filmmaker—writing, shooting, and editing his own movies.

His day job taught him something else, too. He wanted to get to know Marcia Griffin, an editorial assistant. Fields had hired Marcia to help out with the extra work. Marcia and George had both been born in Modesto, although Marcia hadn't grown up there. They both loved movies, and there was definitely a mutual attraction. Finally, the painfully shy George asked Marcia to go with him to a screening of a friend's film.

"It wasn't a real date," he said. "But it was the first time we were ever alone together."

George's nighttime teaching job gave him a chance to present his dump-the-rulebook philosophy to the navy camera operators. He also had time to work on a movie project he was developing, *THX 1138:4EB*. When the navy course was over, George stayed at USC to begin work on his master's degree. He edited *THX* and other films of his own, as well as classmates' films.

Screenings of USC student films were open to the public. Most professional filmmakers did not take these films seriously, although a few studio executives were beginning to keep tabs on the new talent coming

When George met Marcia Griffin, he discovered they had more in common than just their jobs.

out of the film schools. But other students were openly impressed by George's films. Steven Spielberg, a student at Long Beach State University, came to see George's films and meet the man who'd made them. Later he said, "I never had seen a film created by a peer that was not of this earth—*THX* created a world that did not exist before George designed it." As for George himself, Spielberg said he reminded him "of Walt Disney's version of a mad scientist."

George's parents came to Los Angeles for a screening of several student films. There sat George Sr. in "Sin City," surrounded by "long-haired hippie kids," as he called them. "Every time one of George's films would come on, the kids would whisper, 'Watch this one, it's George's film,'" George Sr. said. "We went out to the car and all over the campus all they were talking about was Lucas's films! Now I had been against this thing of his going to the cinema school from day one, but we guessed he had finally found his niche. As we drove home, I said to Dorothy, 'I think we put our money on the right horse.'"

George's older sister Kate, who had once thought her brother was a total loss, changed her mind. "He's a great example for parents not to lose their cool," she said. "I'm just amazed that a person that was so un-together could turn out to be so together."

In the summer of 1967, George was one of four student filmmakers invited to make a short promotional film about the making of a movie called *McKenna's*

Gold. That movie, a Western, would be shot on location in Utah and Arizona.

Before he left Los Angeles, George applied for a Warner Brothers scholarship. Winning the scholarship would enable him to observe a big studio's operation for six months in whatever department he chose. It was a great opportunity. George's friend Walter Murch also applied. They made a pact that whoever won would help the other break into professional filmmaking.

GEORGE'S EARLY PROJECTS

efore leaving the graduate degree program at USC, George made four films:
- *The Emperor,* a documentary about a disc jockey who calls himself Emperor Hudson. Lucas broke the rules by putting the credits in the middle of the film and running sporadic commercials throughout.
- *Herbie,* a series of images of mysterious, gleaming surfaces that are revealed at the end to be a Volkswagen. The title comes from the sound track, which featured the music of renowned jazz musician Herbie Hancock.
- *1:42:08,* about a car race. The title comes from the winning car's time.
- *Anyone Lived in a Pretty How Town,* based on a poem by e. e. cummings.

If George did win, he would be able to stay close to Marcia. This was important to him because their relationship had become serious—they had recently begun living together.

In Arizona, George could scarcely believe the way a big movie studio operated. The director waited until the light was just right before shooting a scene and only then did the cast rehearse the scene—wasting time and money, George thought. He went off by himself to make his film *6.18.67*. It was to be a sort of visual poem or impression of the desert, named for the day it was shot. Even though he'd been hired to capture some aspect of the filming of *McKenna's Gold*, George focused instead on the natural life of the desert. The three other students' films were promotional—they showed the director directing, the wranglers taking care of the horses, the producer at work.

The other students thought George was standoffish, a loner. Certainly George was a private person. But something else was going on with him, too. He missed Marcia. He wrote to her, "This film is going to be a film about you because no matter what I'm photographing, I pretend and wish that it is you."

George returned from Arizona in July. He was happy to come home to the life he shared with Marcia. He entered his films in the National Student Film Festival, the major showcase for student work. He won prizes in three categories—*THX* won top prize for drama, *The Emperor* won an honorable mention for documentary film, and *6.18.67* won for experimental film. George hadn't entered an animated film. Classmate John Milius took that prize for *Marcello, I'm So Bored,* a film that George had edited.

More good news arrived—George had won the Warner Brothers scholarship. This was a big break. The scholarship would be a way into the studio system, where who you knew was what mattered most. John Milius explained the studio system of the time: "There were walls up in Hollywood then, and the place was very cliquish. Movie deals were made at parties. . . . There were parties for people on the A list and for the less important ones on the B List." Few, if any, student filmmakers were on either list. Thus, few young filmmakers had access to a movie deal.

Getting a studio deal meant that a filmmaker would be given the money and resources needed to make a feature film. Feature films were usually about two hours long and intended for widespread release in movie theaters across the country and around the world. They were also very expensive to make. With no financial backing from a studio, independent film-makers had to find ways to come up with the money on their own or through loans.

As unimpressed with Hollywood as George had been, once he won the Warner Brothers scholarship, he was willing to take another look.

Like father, like son—Francis Ford Coppola's son jokes around with some stage costumes.

Chapter **FOUR**

FUTURE VISIONS

GEORGE SHOWED UP AT WARNER BROTHERS IN JULY 1967, decked out in his college sweater instead of his usual outfit of jeans, T-shirt, and sneakers. He headed for the animation department, famous for its Bugs Bunny and Looney Tunes cartoons.

There, George hoped he would see what Hollywood could do in a medium he respected. In animation, everything that appears on the screen has been put there intentionally. No actor's performance can make or break an animated film. Sound and image alone have to work effectively to make a point or drive a story.

When George arrived at the department, he found it had closed. In fact, the whole building was eerily quiet. The studio had been sold to another company.

Jack Warner, the man who had founded Warner Brothers, had just cleaned out his desk and left the day George arrived.

George adjusted to the abrupt shift in the possibilities he'd imagined for his internship. He wandered around before finally heading for the back lot, where a screen adaptation of a Broadway musical, *Finian's Rainbow*, was being shot. George's USC classmate Howard Kazanjian was working there as second assistant to the film's director—Francis Ford Coppola. George was excited. He said, "Francis was the great white knight. He was the one who had made it. He was the one who made us hope."

On the set, George instantly spotted Coppola, a big man with a dark, bushy beard. Coppola spotted George, too. Twenty-two-year-old George was one of the few people on the set who was even close to Coppola's age, twenty-seven. Nearly everyone else was around fifty. "You always feel uncomfortable when there's a stranger watching you," Coppola said. "So I went up to him and asked who he was."

Coppola asked, "See anything interesting?"

George shook his head, waved his hand, palm down, and said, "Not yet."

His brash approach worked. Coppola was that way himself, and not at all opposed to befriending a young filmmaker who showed the same kind of promise he had shown. Coppola took George under his wing, started calling him "the kid," and gave him jobs to do around the set. He eventually made George an administrative assistant. When *Finian's Rainbow* was done, Coppola talked the studio into giving George a contract to expand his student film *THX* into a feature film. He also gave George a job on his next picture, *The Rain People*.

By Thanksgiving of 1967, George wasn't heading back to grad school but rather to New York to join a small crew working for Coppola. Although he didn't like having to be apart from Marcia, who had her own work to do in Los Angeles, George was excited about working for Coppola. After the New York shoot, the crew went on the road to complete filming. George grew a beard when Coppola told him that people respected a bearded man more. "We actually had a lot of fun on that trip," George recalled. "It was rugged, but for all us young clowns, it was a great time." It was rugged because his day started early. At 4:00 A.M., George began working on the expanded script for *THX*. Then, at 7:00 A.M., he went to work for Coppola, helping the camera operator, the sound man, the art director, or whoever needed help. His day ended at 10:00 or 11:00 P.M.

His days were full, but George found something else to fit into them. He thought that Coppola's work was perfect material for a documentary film about the reality of movie production. Coppola agreed that it sounded interesting, so he looted the movie's still-photography budget—$12,000—to pay for George's film stock. His only condition was that George stay out of the way. With this go-ahead, George began to lug around a heavy 16-millimeter camera and a tape recorder, filming Coppola's spontaneous, frantic directing style. George called the result *Filmmaker: a diary by george lucas.*

Even though he was busy, George missed Marcia a lot. In February 1968, she came for a visit. On a train to one of the filming locations, George proposed to her. The two planned to marry as soon as *The Rain People* wrapped up.

Shortly after Marcia had gone back to work in Los Angeles, crew for *The Rain People* arrived in Ogallala, Nebraska, for the end of principal photography—the raw film footage that would later be edited into the final release print. The crew would be in Ogallala for five weeks, and the film's editor, Barry Malkin, needed help organizing the footage. George told Coppola that his girlfriend, Marcia Griffin, was a good assistant editor. Coppola told him to bring her out. Elated, George phoned Marcia to tell her about the five-week job, only to learn that she'd been offered a six-to-nine-month job as assistant editor on Haskell Wexler's movie *Medium Cool.* It would be Marcia's first feature film credit—a big step up and a long-term job. She said she'd have to think about it.

But she didn't think long. She said later, "We were engaged, we were terribly in love, so I decided to go." As it turned out, Marcia was able to work on *Medium Cool* later anyway, so her decision didn't jeopardize her editing career.

The Rain People crew stayed at the Lakeway Lodge in Ogallala. The town even offered to turn an abandoned grain warehouse into a soundstage for Coppola.

The notion of forming a young, one-for-all and all-for-one filmmaker community appealed to Coppola. "We don't have to make films in Hollywood. We can be anywhere in the world we want to be," he said. He envisioned a beautiful, free, artistic life. George saw the dream as a way to reunite USC's Dirty Dozen, with all their camaraderie and artistic passion.

Then, at a 1968 conference of English teachers in San Francisco, George took Coppola's place as a speaker in a panel discussion, and he met someone who was living just such a dream. Panelist John Korty had started as a documentary director. In 1964, he'd moved to Stinson Beach, a secluded area north of San Francisco, and rented a barn for $100 a month. There he'd made three feature films in four years. All three films together had cost only $250,000—much less than the average cost of a single feature film produced by a studio. Korty, one of the most successful independent directors in the country, had proven that the dream could be a reality.

After the panel discussion, George grabbed Korty, dragged him to a pay phone, and called Coppola in Ogallala. "Listen to John Korty," George shouted. "He's *doing* what we've been talking about!" George and Coppola arranged to see Korty's studio that summer.

Before then, George had something even more important to do—get married to Marcia. The ceremony took place on February 22, 1969, at the United First Methodist Church in Pacific Grove, California. The couple honeymooned in Northern California. They especially liked Marin County, north of San Francisco. They decided to settle there. Marcia found a small house for rent in Mill Valley, and the Lucases moved in.

While Marcia looked around for editing work in San Francisco, George continued working on *THX*. He and Coppola visited John Korty's studio on July 4, 1969— Independence Day in more ways than one. "They were amazed to see that I had an editing table, everything I needed," Korty said. "Francis said, 'If you can do it, I can do it.'"

George and Marcia sometimes worked together on projects before and after they were married.

Inspired, Coppola went to Europe to visit other film studios. Lanterna Films in Denmark especially impressed him. The beautiful mansion converted into a studio sat in the country, fifty miles from Copenhagen. This was the atmosphere Coppola wanted to create in Northern California. He also stopped at a film trade show (an exhibition of filmmaking materials and equipment) in Germany and bought sound-mixing equipment. Then he returned to California to look for a Victorian mansion to buy in Marin County. But bids on three houses fell through, and the equipment would be arriving any day from Europe. When Korty finally found an empty warehouse at 827 Folsom Street in San Francisco, Coppola and George rented it.

Coppola was president of the new venture, and George was vice president. The two men were total opposites in personality. Where Coppola was talkative and lively, Lucas was reserved. "I was always putting on the brakes and he was always stepping on the gas," George said. But they complemented each other, and it looked like all systems go for the venture.

George suggested they call the new company Transamerican Sprocket Works. Sprockets are the slots on the edges of celluloid film that guide it through a projector. But Coppola wanted a different name—American Zoetrope. A zoetrope is an early moving-picture device that projects images when its cylinder is spun.

The new company became a legal reality on November 14, 1969. The sound equipment arrived, carpenters worked to partition the office spaces, and John Korty moved in as the company's first official tenant. The grapevine to USC and UCLA soon brought in other tenants.

When the place was in working order, Coppola went to Warner Brothers to ask for financing to develop scripts and film them. The studio had been acquired by a parking lot company and was headed by former talent agent Ted Ashley. Coppola promised Ashley that American Zoetrope could script and produce five films for $3.5 million. Ashley agreed, but added that if no finished movies resulted, Zoetrope would have to repay any development money it had spent.

One of those five films was *THX*, and it was not going well. In George's opinion, rewrites by Coppola and writer Oliver Hailey didn't improve the script. When Walter Murch arrived to edit sound effects for *The Rain People*, George asked him to help with *THX*, but the script still wasn't coming together. George turned his attention to another project, a film about Vietnam that he had discussed with John Milius, called *Apocalypse Now*. George asked Milius to help him write a treatment, or short description, of that film.

But Coppola wasn't ready to let *THX* go. He made an impressive sales pitch to Warner Brothers, tossing in the Vietnam idea that George and Milius were working on. He came away with a budget of $777,777.77 to produce *THX*. Seven was his lucky number.

George was happy about *THX*, but upset because

Captain Buck Rogers looks over a futuristic gizmo in the television series based on the famed comic book hero.

Coppola had thrown in *Apocalypse Now*, which he had not been involved with up to this point. Still, it looked like Zoetrope was on its feet, and that was good. George swallowed his irritation over *Apocalypse Now* and returned to work on *THX*.

Set in the twenty-fifth century, *THX-1138* opens with a clip from an old Buck Rogers movie serial, over which a voice says, "There's nothing supernatural or mystic: take Buck, he's just an ordinary human being who keeps his wits about him." In George's own words, the message of *THX* is, "If you want something bad enough, you can do it. We are living in cages with the doors open."

The film was released in 1971, a time of social and political turbulence in the United States. "Modern society is a rotten thing," George said at the time. "If you're smart, you'll . . . start an alternative civilization above ground, out of the sewer you find yourself in." Students put it more succinctly: "Turn on, tune in, drop out." *THX* reflects George's view of an individual pitted against the masses, a classic science fiction theme.

The title character is a man who is known only as a number, THX 1138. He lives in a bleached-out, subterranean future where the government doles out sedatives and provides mindlessly violent holographic television programs. THX works in a robot factory and lives with a computer-selected roommate, LUH 3417. Although sexuality is banned, the two fall in love. Enter SEN 5241, a middle-aged man who has lost his roommate. SEN illegally rigs the computer to allow him to live with THX, casting LUH aside. She's in trouble anyway because she is pregnant, which is also a crime. All three are found out, and ruthless robot police seize them. SEN and THX try to escape. They run into a holographic character who has always wanted to be real and is also fleeing. The three discover that LUH's number has been reassigned to a bottled fetus in a lab. They understand that she's been eliminated. SEN chooses the familiar over freedom and goes back. The hologram's car crashes, leaving THX to make his way to the earth's surface alone. When his car runs out of road, THX continues on foot, past the stinking, dwarfish shell-dwellers and up a final chimney. He emerges on the surface to stand against a giant desert sun. A bird flies by.

George had a short shooting schedule of ten weeks to make *THX*. Filming began at the end of 1969. He would film with Techniscope, an older film process he'd learned about at USC. It was quick to set up, used half as much film as newer processes, and, when used with normal camera lenses, it yielded a wide-screen effect. For his first feature film, George wanted to use available light as much as possible and to film on existing locations rather than build elaborate sets. He shot in unfinished San Francisco subway tunnels and outside futuristic-looking buildings.

George had studio money to work with and almost limitless creative control over the film. His friend and cowriter Walter Murch created the sound effects—bleeps, bloops, and broadcast messages offering "the blessing of the State, the blessing of the Masses" and urging everyone to "Buy, Be Happy!" Murch's sound effects evolved to fit what George shot, and Murch used his own voice as the Voice of God. Lalo Schifrin's musical score grew out of George's question, "What would the Muzak of the future be like?" Schifrin said, "I had to write . . . purposely stupid music."

George lucked into a fine cast—Robert Duvall as THX 1138, Maggie McOmie as LUH 3417, Donald

Pleasance as SEN 5241—selected by Coppola's associate Ron Colby. These performers did not need a lot of direction. George was glad. "I'm not very good with people. . . . It's a real weak link for me," he said.

He got the message that he was a cold fish at the end of the shoot, when Coppola set up a group therapy session with the producers, the director, and the crew to wind things up and provide a framework for personal growth. George learned that he'd have to get past his detachment from people to work effectively in the movie business, but it was hard for him, perhaps impossible. Years later, actor Mark Hamill said, "I have a sneaking suspicion that if there were a way to make movies without actors, George would do it."

For George, the first five minutes and the last twenty minutes of a film were all that counted. The rest was filler. If the filler had enough action, he thought, the audience wouldn't notice if the characters were weak. Trained in technology, George was more attuned to film technique than to film as story.

The year following the filming of *THX* was dedicated to postproduction—editing the footage and creating and tweaking the sound. George, Marcia, and Murch worked in shifts in the attic and extra bedroom of the Lucases' Mill Valley house. One day, another USC graduate, Gary Kurtz, came to discuss the Techniscope process. While Kurtz was there, he and George began toying with the idea of a film set in the late '50s or early '60s. They imagined a "feel-good," pre-Beatles rock and roll movie about an innocent time before the assassination of President Kennedy and the war in Vietnam. It sounded like a promising idea, but first George had to finish *THX*.

When it was done, Coppola came to see it. "Strange, strange," he muttered. The next day, he flew to Los Angeles with George's movie and scripts he and others at Zoetrope had worked on. When the studio executives saw *THX*, they demanded that Coppola turn it over to them for editing. Coppola did as they asked— they had, after all, paid for the film. Warner Brothers rejected the other scripts and demanded that Zoetrope repay the $300,000 the studio had spent on them.

Back in San Francisco, Coppola announced the bad news on what the people involved called Black Thursday. Coppola struggled to repay Warner Brothers any way he could. He raised John Korty's rent abruptly from $200 to $1,000 a month. Tenants fled like mice before the exterminator. When Paramount Pictures asked Coppola to direct *The Godfather,* a story about the Italian mafia in the United States, the job promised a way out of financial disaster. George encouraged Coppola to do the movie and later helped film the gang wars for *The Godfather.* The film became one of the highest-grossing movies of all time, reversing Coppola's money woes handsomely.

George began developing the rock and roll screenplay he had discussed with Gary Kurtz. In the meantime, Warner Brothers cut five minutes from *THX* and

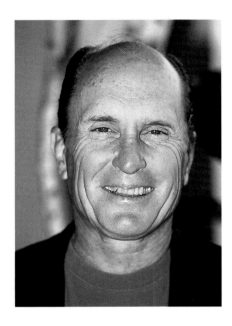

A young Robert Duvall played the starring role in the second version of THX-1138.

released it with no fanfare. Ticket buyers showed little interest in the film.

Critical response was mixed. Film critics praised the atmosphere and action but considered the dialogue and characterizations weak. Some critics pointed out that the film's assertion that people only have to take the first step to get out of whatever trap they're in isn't true for everybody. Not all people are white, middle-class sons of California businessmen, they said. Some people *are* caged by poverty or other life circumstances.

Already emotionally vulnerable at the thought that his film had crashed Zoetrope, George was even more upset when reviewers speculated that the creator of *THX* must be a cold person. George lashed back, calling critics "the vandals of our time, like spray-painters who mess up walls." It angered him that critics spent less than a day thinking and writing about films that took two or three years to make. "I basically said, 'To hell with reviews.'"

Even though *THX* didn't sell many tickets, George said, "It was the only movie I really enjoyed doing. It's always a big thrill doing your first film because you haven't gone through the other end of it, all the criticism, anguish, and failure. That doesn't even occur to you because you don't know what can go wrong. It's all fun."

George has always been very active in protecting the copyrights of his movies.

Chapter **FIVE**

WHERE WERE YOU IN '62?

IT WAS 1970. GEORGE WAS TWENTY-FIVE YEARS OLD and once again pondering his future. The American Zoetrope dream was dead, and he wasn't able to proceed with writing the "Flash Gordon space thing" he had in mind. Italian director Federico Fellini had already bought the rights to use that material from Alex Raymond, the author of the Flash Gordon books. George couldn't use it without breaking copyright law, which protects creative works such as books, songs, and movies.

Copyright protection is important. Artistic works belong to the people who create them, unless they choose to sell or give the rights to someone else, often for adaptation in other media. Ownership of creative works is akin to ownership of products like cars—you can't go out and sell somebody else's car to a third person without arranging for the transfer of the car's legal title. Ownership of creative works can be more complicated, however. Who owns a marble sculpture? The artist who made it, the collector who bought it, or the museum that displays it? In filmmaking, dozens of people collaborate on a project, and ownership of ideas is a murky area of the law.

By 1970, some good things were happening for George. He'd found an agent and a lawyer. George's new lawyer was Tom Pollock. His new agent was Jeff Berg, who worked for Creative Management Associates, the agency that also represented director John Milius, the husband-and-wife writing team of Willard Huyck and Gloria Katz, and director Matthew Robbins. An agent's job is to place an idea or creative work with a publisher, art gallery, or producer. They negotiate contracts for clients, trying to get the best possible financial arrangement, and they make sure the terms of the contract are fulfilled.

George had an idea besides the stalled "Flash Gordon space thing"—the rock and roll film he and Gary Kurtz had discussed. George thought that a film portraying life as it was in Modesto in the '50s when he was a teen would appeal to people of his generation. They were the audience buying most of the movie tickets—and ticket sales were important. *THX* hadn't made money, and because it wasn't a commercial success, the studios had pigeonholed George as a non-commercial filmmaker. They were leery of putting money into his projects.

But George pushed on. "MUSICAL," he wrote at the top of his five-page treatment for the movie he called *American Graffiti*. But this film wasn't the usual kind of musical, in which people break into song and dance at the drop of a hat. Instead, in *American Graffiti*, "the dancing is created by cars performing a fifties ritual called Cruising. An endless parade of kids bombing around in dagoed, moondisked, flamed, chopped, tuck-and-rolled machines rumbling through a seemingly adultless, heat-drugged little town. . . . The passing chrome-flashing cars become a visual choreography."

George's agent tried to sell the treatment to studios all over Hollywood. They all rejected it. The Lucases were down to their last $2,000—Marcia's savings. Things looked bleak. Then George and Marcia learned that the Cannes Film Festival, a world-renowned film festival held each year in Cannes, France, had set up a showcase for new directors called Directors Fortnight. *THX* was one of the scheduled films. The Lucases decided to go for broke. They headed for Europe in May 1970 with their backpacks and sleeping bags. First they stopped in New York City, where the president of the United Artists studio, David Picker, was based. United Artists vice president David Chasman had already rejected *American Graffiti*, but George

Considered classics now, these cars were like the ones George grew up with.

decided to go over Chasman's head and show the treatment to Picker.

Surprisingly, Picker said he would read it. He told George he would call him with his decision. The Lucases went on to London, where, on May 14, George's twenty-sixth birthday, he heard from Picker. Picker said he'd give George $10,000 to develop the treatment into a full-fledged script. George immediately phoned Gary Kurtz, whom he had asked to produce the film. Kurtz said he'd take care of the script. He phoned screenwriters Huyck and Katz, but they were busy working on a horror flick, *Messiah of Evil.* Kurtz found another writer.

Meanwhile, George and Marcia saw *THX* in Cannes. It was a hit, selling out both of its screenings. Heartened, they bought a Eurail train pass and toured the European racing car circuit from Le Mans to the Monaco Grand Prix before coming home.

Back home, George eagerly read the finished script

for *American Graffiti.* It was all wrong! It was incorrect about drag racing and overtly sexual. Worse, the writer had already been paid the whole $10,000.

Now the Lucases were down to $500. George had no choice but to write another draft of *Graffiti* himself. As he labored over several drafts, time passed and money ran out. He and Marcia were forced to borrow from his parents, other relatives, and friends.

United Artists kept rejecting George's drafts of the movie. Money, or the lack of it, had become a real problem for George and Marcia. But Tom Pollock, George's lawyer, set up a company, Lucasfilm Ltd., to contract out George's directing services. An independent production company offered George $100,000 to direct a film. He read the script and didn't like it. He conferred with Marcia, and she agreed that he should turn down the job, even though they were broke.

Betting on his own instincts and intuitions as always, George was convinced the time was right for a film like *American Graffiti.* He called his close friends Willard Huyck and Gloria Katz to help him write it. They had finished *The Evil Messiah,* so they could work on *American Graffiti* to bring the characters and dialogue to life.

George's agent made another stab at selling this version of the script to a studio. Ned Tanen, a young executive at Universal Studios, was willing to give George a chance, but Tanen needed to know that the film would make money. Get a name like Coppola involved, he said, and toss in the "Flash Gordon thing." Both requirements were met, so it was a deal—except for the title. *American Graffiti,* both Tanen and Coppola said, sounded like an Italian movie about feet. George stood firm. He wanted to evoke memories of a vanished civilization, and he felt that was what his title plainly said.

American Graffiti is the story of a pivotal night in the lives of four buddies aged seventeen to twenty. Two of them, Steve and Curt, are about to leave their small hometown for college. Both have doubts. Steve, the blond, athletic former class president, ends up staying. Brainy Curt goes. The other two guys' lives revolve around cars. The oldest is "greaser" Milner, who wants to be drag-race king of the road forever. The other is Terry the Toad, described in the treatment as "sixteen long years of being a short loser." While George's friend Walter Murch has said that all four characters represent different parts of George, George himself said he was really only two of them—Terry, the shy nerd who's the butt of everybody's jokes, and Curt.

The film opens with an orange bar moving from side to side. The camera pulls back slowly to reveal that the bar is a car radio dial. Legendary disc jockey Wolfman Jack spins rock and roll music throughout the film. As critics Michael Pye and Lynda Myles point out, the film's music covers at least a decade's worth of tunes, from the '50s sound of Buddy Holly to the '60s surfing sound of the Beach Boys.

The deep and scratchy voice of Wolfman Jack became part of the "soup of sound" in American Graffiti.

All night long, the cars cruise. Occasionally they stop at Mel's Drive-In for a burger or to shift passengers. The driving seems aimless, but there's a goal—to find girls. And there are girls in the film—Laurie, Debbie, Carol, and a nameless blond in a white T-bird.

The drag-racing accident that happens in *American Graffiti* echoed George's experience, as well as that of many other teens. The film is a distillation of teen experience, focusing on the uncertainty and pain of the changes everybody has to go through to grow up. The universality of these events and the sound track's rock and roll music allowed even viewers who hadn't grown up in the United States to identify with the film.

Coppola suggested that George hire Fred Roos, who had cast most of *The Godfather,* to help cast *Graffiti.* "We decided to make a massive search for good kids, and that's what it was, massive; it went on for weeks and months," Roos said.

American Graffiti was inspired by life in Modesto, but that town had grown too large to film the movie there. Nearby San Rafael looked right, but trouble began even before the twenty-eight-day shoot was scheduled to start—June 26, 1972. The day before, a key crew member was arrested for possessing marijuana. The second day, cast and crew arrived to find their filming permit revoked by the town. A bar owner said the production blocked access to his business. Kurtz negotiated a compromise. They would film in San Rafael three more nights, then move to Petaluma. The deal settled, filming went on for an hour—until a restaurant burst into flames and the town's main street was closed to make room for the fire trucks. When George moved the filming to the town's back streets, an assistant cameraman fell off the camera car. No serious injuries, but time was lost.

As the shoot went on, other problems surfaced. George had collected vintage '50s cars from all over northern California. The latter-day "greasers" driving them roared around town, drinking beer and disturbing the citizens. George's sleep was disturbed for a different reason. He wasn't a night person, but filming had to be done at night, so he was getting only two or three hours of sleep a day. His difficulties in relating to people in general and actors in particular added to his stress.

George once described his emotional state while

directing by referring to the needle on a sound meter that moves in response to volume and intensity. What happened to him, George said, "is the needle starts out at zero, and two days into shooting it's up in the red—and it just stays in the red."

George was soon bleary-eyed and in generally poor health. And still more problems plagued the filming. He had thought he could both direct and oversee the photography, so he tried to save money by hiring two local camera operators instead of Hollywood pro-fessionals. This wasn't working. Cameraman Haskell Wexler offered to help, but there wasn't any budget left to pay him, and he was filming commercials all day in Los Angeles. But Wexler was a longtime friend. He said he'd fly up at night and help for no pay.

After dinner most nights, Wexler flew to San Francisco and met a helicopter that took him to Sausalito, where a car picked him up to drive him to the Petaluma lo-cation. He wasn't getting any more sleep than George was. But unlike George, Wexler was energized by the enthusiasm of the *Graffiti* cast and crew. And he knew how to get the neon, jukebox look that George wanted for the film. Wexler lighted the actors inside their cars with subdued recreational-vehicle lights taped under the roofs. He also jacked up a truck and turned its head-lights on and off to give the illusion of passing cars on the actors' faces.

August 4, 1972, was the last day of filming. It was time to add music and sound effects and to edit the

THE CAST OF AMERICAN GRAFFITI

Curt Henderson. This was Richard Dreyfuss's first starring role. Later, he'd appear in Steven Spielberg's *Jaws* and *Close Encounters of the Third Kind* and win an Oscar for his role in *The Goodbye Girl.*

Steve Bolander. Eighteen years old when he auditioned, Ron Howard was still considered a child actor because of his role as Opie on television's *The Andy Griffith Show;* he later played Ritchie Cunningham on television's *Happy Days.* Howard later directed *Willow* as well as several other films for Lucasfilm.

John Milner. Actor Paul LeMat, a one-time professional boxer, later appeared in the television series *Lonesome Dove.*

Terry (the Toad) Fields. Actor/writer/director Charles Martin Smith came out of the audition process, one of the few *Graffiti* actors unknown to casting director Roos.

Laurie. Cindy Williams went on to star in television's *Laverne & Shirley* series.

Debbie. Candy Clark received an Oscar nomination for Best Supporting Actress for her role in *Graffiti.* The Oscar went to another actress. Clark later played in Lucasfilm's *Radioland Murders.*

Carol. Twelve-year-old Mackenzie Philips, who later starred in the *One Day at a Time* television series, was the only cast member Lucas had qualms about. She was underage, covered by California child-labor laws. Coproducer Kurtz became her legal guardian during production.

Wolfman Jack. He played himself, a role he later reprised on television and in films.

Bob Falfa. Harrison Ford earned a living as a carpenter during lean spells in his acting career. He later starred as Han Solo and Indiana Jones. Nominated for a Best Actor Oscar for *Witness* in 1985, he won a People's Choice Award as Most Popular Actor in 1998.

Joe. Actor Bo Hopkins later played in *Radioland Murders.*

footage into its final form. Walter Murch came to work on the sound. Earlier, Universal had refused George's request for $10,000 to buy the rights to the copyrighted songs he wanted to use on the sound track. Although he'd had to pare down his list from eighty to forty-five songs, there was still plenty of music to achieve what Murch called a "soup of sound"—the music plus all the sound effects. George and Murch created the sound in stereo, with complex cutting between speakers at the front and back of movie theaters as well as from side to side.

Marcia Lucas and Verna Fields began to edit the film, working in a two-story garage behind the house Coppola had bought in Mill Valley at George's urging. Lucas looked at the edited footage every day and gave instructions. That was all the time George and Marcia could find to spend together.

The cut film ran two hours and forty-five minutes— forty-five minutes too long. Most feature films are no more than two hours long. George's attempts to shorten *American Graffiti* left it disjointed and choppy. Verna Fields had gone on to other work, so Marcia stepped in to deftly cut the film to just under two hours while George went back to working on sound with Murch. Finally the film was ready for its first sneak preview.

The screening was held on Sunday, January 28, 1973, in the North Point area of San Francisco. The film broke twice in the first ten minutes, and the sound wasn't in sync, but the eight hundred people in the theater cheered anyway.

When the film ended, its makers were elated. But studio executive Ned Tanen wasn't impressed. Minutes earlier, he had sputtered to Kurtz, "It's unreleasable! A disaster!" Now Tanen told Coppola, "I went to bat for you and you let me down!"

George stood there in shock, but Coppola shouted back at Kurtz, "You should get down on your knees and thank George for saving your job!" George had almost killed himself making this film, Coppola continued. George had brought it in on time and on budget. Coppola threatened to buy the movie back right then and there if Kurtz didn't want it.

A crowd gathered. Kurtz tried to calm things down. He said he and George would make a list of possible changes based on the tape recording he'd made of the audience's reaction during the screening. They could meet the next day to discuss the changes.

Steven Spielberg wasn't at the screening, but he said he wished he had been. He called the incident "the best story to come out of Hollywood since the late 1940s." It marked the difference between the Old Hollywood, in which the studios held all the power and could make or break an artist's career, and the New Hollywood of the young, film-school-trained directors.

At the meeting the day after the screening, Tanen brought his own list of changes he wanted. To start, he wanted the film to be shorter. But because of a

Writers Guild strike, Coppola and George, who were both guild members, were not allowed to work at the studios. Universal was free to do what it wanted. It cut five minutes and the stereo sound from the film. Kurtz was not a Writers Guild member, however, so he could still work with Tanen to save the film from being dropped altogether.

George, Coppola, Kurtz, and Tanen all fought for the movie. They filled the studio previews with young secretaries and kids—normally, previews were attended only by studio executives. Even after seeing the young people's enthusiasm, the executives left the previews asking what the film was about. What did the title mean? Someone suggested the movie might be all right for television, a market the studio was actively courting. No one knew what to do with the film.

But all the arguing stopped on August 1, 1973, when *American Graffiti* opened at the Avco Theater in Westwood, near the UCLA campus. Universal had finally released the film after learning that Alan Ladd Jr., an executive at rival studio 20th Century Fox, had seen a pirated copy of the film and was interested.

Some reviewers raved. The *Los Angeles Times* called *American Graffiti* "one of the most important films of the year, as well as the one most likely to move you to tears." But Pauline Kael, a writer for *The New Yorker* magazine and the dean of American film critics, blasted the film. Of its nostalgia, she wrote, "For whom was it 'just like that,' I wonder. Not for women, not for blacks or Orientals or Puerto Ricans, not for homosexuals, not for the poor. Only for white middle-class boys whose memories have turned into pop."

Unlike Kael, many moviegoers found the film's sub-urban values of the '50s reassuring, especially during the social turmoil of the '70s, when college campuses were rife with protest over the war in Vietnam. But it was true that *American Graffiti* lacked a broader awareness of social issues and could be seen as sexist. For example, although the film tells what happened to each of the four young men, viewers learn nothing about the girls' fate at film's end.

Huyck and Katz had argued with George about the ending while they were working on the script, but George said he'd made a "filmic decision." He'd started by writing a screenplay about four guys, so the film should end with them, even though their stories were interwoven with the girls' stories. "My usual problem of sacrificing content for form," George later said.

Whatever its problems, the film's collage of nostalgic music brought the cruising ritual back to life for a huge audience. The movie influenced many other movies and television shows. The '70s television series *Happy Days* and *Laverne & Shirley* spun off from *American Graffiti,* as did films like *Grease.* The enter-tainment industry learned from *American Graffiti* to weave multiple, unrelated story lines together. Many television series, including *Homicide* and *NYPD Blue,* use that technique.

The television series Laverne & Shirley *was one of several shows inspired by* American Graffiti.

Graffiti earned more than $50 million for Universal. Made on a $750,000 budget, the film was "possibly the biggest return on investment in Hollywood's modern history," according to former *Los Angeles Times* film critic Charles Champlin.

American Graffiti made George a multimillionaire years ahead of his thirtieth birthday, more than fulfilling the prediction he'd shouted at his father before going to film school. George shared the wealth. He gave cars or money to some people who had contributed to the film. To others he gave points—a percentage of the net profits after studio deductions had been made for filming and distributing the movie. The points George handed out made a number of their recipients millionaires as well.

Francis Coppola had been guaranteed a percentage of the profits when he signed the contract to produce the film. From the beginning, he'd balked at sharing his profits with the film's other producer, Gary Kurtz, saying he hadn't hired Kurtz. Coppola also complained about sharing the profits with Wexler, who had worked for free and had contributed enormously to the film. When the money started coming in, George paid Kurtz and Wexler promptly, but Coppola paid them only after intense negotiations.

Coppola and George, unlikely partners to begin with, drifted apart. Further wrangles a year later over who would make *Apocalypse Now* led George to put even more distance between them. Coppola made the film. "And then we had to go our separate ways," George said later. Over time, Coppola and George came together again to jointly support a number of films, including *Mishima, Captain EO, Tucker: The Man and His Dream,* and *Powaqqatsi.* They also worked together in 1980 to support Japanese director Akira Kurosawa in making *Kagemusha.*

George's *Graffiti* earnings—$4 million after taxes—did not come in until months after the film opened. Until then, the Lucases were dependent on Marcia's editing income and more loans. When financial success did begin to trickle in, the Lucases repaid the money they'd borrowed and moved to a small home in San Anselmo, California. They made only one really major purchase—a dilapidated wood-frame Victorian house built in 1869, which they bought in December 1973 for $150,000. Marcia named the house Parkhouse. It was George's version of the Zoetrope dream. He added on a screening room and a writing room to the house, and the bedrooms became offices for the staff of Lucasfilm Ltd., the company his lawyer had set up in

1970. The company had grown to include five staff people, including Kurtz.

With his *Graffiti* profits, George would never have to work again if he didn't want to. But for George, money was not all important. "There's never been a period when money was a major focus for me," he said. He had other goals. He wanted to do a full-scale production and keep total control of it. His experience with both *THX* and *American Graffiti* had taught him that movie studios could grab control and change his films. They could violate his vision.

John Korty has said that for George, things are either totally dark or totally light. Interfering with a creative work was dark. The outcome of the battles of his next film might take care of both fictional and real-life evils.

George believed space should have sound in the movies. With this in mind, he designed the sound effects for his set pieces, like the space cruiser in the background.

Chapter **SIX**

A HERO'S JOURNEY

GEORGE HAD A HUNCH THAT AUDIENCES WOULD LEAVE the comforts of home to see movies that the whole family could enjoy, like an update of the old Flash Gordon serials. But since he'd been unable to get those movie rights in 1973, he began to research other materials he could use to make a "real, gee-whiz movie," a high adventure. He said, "I watched kids' movies, and how they work and how myths work; and I looked very carefully at the elements of films within that fairy-tale genre which made them successful."

In *The Hero with a Thousand Faces* and other books, philosopher Joseph Campbell identified a series of elements in the hero's journey, a framework found in myths and stories around the world. Campbell says that heroes typically cross a threshold from the ordinary world into an extraordinary one, where they grow emotionally and spiritually by being tested. They survive, learn, and finally return home to enrich their society by sharing their new-found knowledge.

George saw great possibilities in telling a hero's story. Letters teenagers wrote to him about *American Graffiti* convinced him that films could make a difference in people's lives. This was important. George had found "no modern mythology to give kids a sense of values, to give them a strong mythological fantasy life."

The idea of crossing the threshold into outer space appealed to George because he believed science-fiction fans would guarantee strong ticket sales. Those sales alone might be enough to cover the cost of making the picture. Anything else would be extra. George considered Stanley Kubrick's elegant 1968 film *2001: A Space Odyssey* "the ultimate science fiction movie." He knew he had to do something different.

Kubrick's space was static and silent, as the laws of physics require it to be. George thought that if he tipped off audiences at the very beginning of his movie that they were watching a fantasy, his version of space could be lively. A symphony could orchestrate star fields. The engine of an Empire cruiser could roar. A Death Star could be blasted. *Once upon a time* could become *A long time ago in a galaxy far, far away.* This film could say what *THX* had said, but in a more positive way.

By May 1973, George had filled thirteen pages of blue-

and-green lined paper with tiny print. It was the treatment of *Star Wars,* and it was hard to read for reasons other than just the size of the letters.

Executives at United Artists—a studio that still had a claim on George's projects—frowned at an opening sentence that read, "The story of Mace Windu, a revered Jedi-bendu of Opuchi who was related to Usby C. J. Thape, paddawaan learner to the famed Jedi." No one knew what George was talking about. United Artists rejected the project. Decision makers at Universal Studios also turned it down. The reader at Universal thought the characters were less interesting than the action and special effects. The reader also expressed doubts in "Mr. Lucas's ability to pull it all off."

But 20th Century Fox development executive Alan Ladd Jr. was keenly interested, especially when George described *Star Wars* as a combination of the Flash Gordon serials and the Errol Flynn swashbuckler movies. Ladd said yes to the project and gave George fifteen thousand dollars to develop the script.

George isolated himself in his room at Parkhouse and wrote eight hours a day, five days a week. On one wall was a photograph of the pioneering Russian film director Sergei Eisenstein. On the opposite wall hung a *THX* poster. There was also a pink and purple Wurlitzer jukebox, but George wouldn't allow himself to play it until he'd written his daily quota of pages. He only quit writing when it was time for the *CBS Evening News* with Walter Cronkite.

George and the little Star Wars *robot R2-D2 meet Walter Cronkite.*

Star Wars is the story of the triumph of a group of dedicated rebels over a repressive empire in space. George borrowed elements from *THX*—the shell-dwellers became Jawas, for example—and also from other science-fiction materials. The diplomatic android C-3PO in *Star Wars* echoes a polite metal man in author Alex Raymond's *Iron Men of Mongo,* and George's banthas are similar to characters in Edgar Rice Burroughs's *John Carter on Mars.* The evil ruler Ming in the Flash Gordon books inspired George's Emperor.

Every weekend, George brought home an armload of comics and science-fiction books. When Marcia asked what he was doing, he said he was planning a movie ten-year-old boys would love.

George also incorporated elements of various religions into his screenplay. Yoda is a Buddhist. The Force is what New Thought Christians or pantheists might call the Unified Field of Consciousness. George said he wanted to impart a spiritual message, to tell viewers that "the laws are really in yourself." In fact,

George's research was so exhaustive and his scripting so inclusive that almost anything can be read into *Star Wars*.

Remembering how much he'd liked cliff-hanger endings as a child, George used them often in *Star Wars*. For example, Luke Skywalker carries his own rope and uses it to swing himself and Princess Leia away from the storm troopers closing in on them in the Imperial hangar.

George carried a notebook to jot down ideas. He wrote one note when he and Walter Murch were mixing the sound for *American Graffiti*. Murch asked George for R2, D2—meaning Reel 2, Dialogue 2. George took note of the abbreviation. In *Star Wars*, it became the name of the squat, cute robot who, along with C-3PO, served as comic relief.

As George worked, he described the story as a space fantasy, instead of a science-fiction movie, hoping to divert attention from the commercial failure of *THX*. "I suppose it's a space fantasy," George wrote to 20th Century Fox. "But we don't explain anything. . . . The story really is an action adventure, a fantasy hero's journey. It's aimed primarily at teenagers, the same audience as *American Graffiti*." The last sentence was meant to remind studio executives that George had already proven that he could reach teenage viewers successfully.

The first draft of *Star Wars* was finished in May 1974; the second draft on January 28, 1975. The third, finished on August 1, 1975, was the first to mention the Force. The fourth draft was completed eight months later. The story and its characters changed and grew, and they continued to do so until the day before filming started, when Luke Starkiller became Luke Skywalker. The writing of *Star Wars* came just as hard for George as the writing of *American Graffiti* had. His eyes blurred behind his horn-rimmed glasses. When frustrated, he would snip off a lock of his hair with a scissors and toss it into a wastebasket.

The script grew to five hundred pages—roughly three hundred and eighty pages longer than the usual screenplay. But it fell into neat divisions, with detailed story lines for not one but three trilogies. Episode IV was the most commercial part of the script. By the time Alan Ladd Jr. at Fox got that portion of the fourth draft in December 1975, Lucas had already spent almost $1 million of his *Graffiti* money on the film's preproduction—all the things that happen in preparation for filming.

One early preproduction cost was Ralph McQuarrie's paintings. Filmmakers of the time used paintings as backgrounds for scenes that were shot on a soundstage inside a studio rather than outdoors on location. Instead of filming actors in a barn or in Tahiti, for example, the director could film them in front of a background painting of a barn wall or a beach in Tahiti.

McQuarrie's paintings were especially crucial for the film as George envisioned it. McQuarrie, an illustrator for Boeing Aircraft, had done paintings of the Apollo space missions. He and George worked together to develop a series of *Star Wars* paintings. The skills George had gained while building his dioramas as a child in Modesto were put to use in imagining the new worlds of *Star Wars*.

The paintings would be used in several ways. First, they could be lined up in sequence to give Fox studio executives an idea of how the finished film would look. More importantly, they could create the illusion of reality through a process called composite photography. For example, a painting of star-filled space would be filmed. Then an X-Wing spacecraft would be filmed, followed by shots of a TIE fighter. The three pieces of film could be condensed into one, showing a TIE fighter attacking the X-Wing in space. By using several different layers of film at once, the filmmakers could show an aerial dogfight.

McQuarrie's paintings were also used to design the storyboard sketches. Storyboards are representations of the scenes that the audience will see in a film. The sketches are drawn in a comic-book style and tell the camera operators exactly what and how to film. The Death Star was actually exploded in a parking lot without the star-filled background as seen in the movie. The sketches were the only guides for filming. Later, the storyboards were used again, when the explosion was joined with a shot of the painting of space to create the finished scene.

George also had to line up a producer, someone who would serve as a business manager for the film on a day-by-day basis. He chose Gary Kurtz, who had produced *Graffiti* and was on the Lucasfilm staff. Kurtz suggested that the soundstage portions of the film be shot in England at Elstree Studios, a thirty-minute drive from London. He and George flew to Europe in May 1975 to look at the studio. While on the trip, they hired Colin Cantwell to design the spaceship models. Cantwell had worked on *2001*.

Back home, Kurtz recruited Ben Burtt, a teaching assistant in USC's sound department. George told Burtt that everything had to sound real, which posed a challenge. "The sounds of the real world are complicated and kind of dirty," Burtt explained. "They simply cannot be reproduced on a synthesizer." He spent a year foraging for real sounds. "I'd call up somebody and say, 'I hear you have a trained bear that makes a funny sound.'" Nothing escaped Burtt's recorder—planes taking off and landing, rusty motors grinding. He created every sound in *Star Wars* except the actors' dialogue and the music. Even the sound of footsteps on metal had to be created because the sets were built of wood.

Later, Burtt mixed his sounds at Sprocket Systems, established in 1975 and later known as Skywalker Sound. Burtt created voices for Chewbacca, R2-D2, and other space creatures. He also created sound effects, achieving the sound of the laser swords by

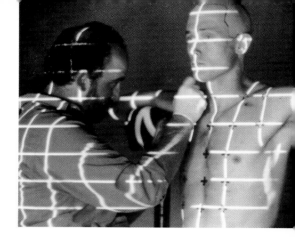

A designer at Industrial Light & Magic works on the special effects for the movie Terminator II.

mixing the hum of movie projectors with static from his television's picture tube.

Kurtz hired another key person, John Dykstra, to make use of the computerized film technology that had blossomed during the 1970s. Kurtz found a warehouse in Van Nuys, California, and Dykstra assembled a technical team to work on the special effects for *Star Wars*. This top-notch group, working out of the warehouse, turned into a division of Lucasfilm Ltd. called Industrial Light & Magic (ILM). ILM also redesigned the spaceship models when Cantwell's models proved much too sleek and NASA-like for George. The ILM staff grew to nearly one hundred people during the filmmaking. The average age of the employees was twenty-seven, and there were no set hours or dress codes. Workers wore jeans or shorts and T-shirts instead of suits and ties.

Producer Gary Kurtz hired Robert Watts to supervise production, the job Watts had on *2001*. And so the creative team was put together. George told everyone that he wanted the look of a future that was dented, rusted, and driven hard. He told composer John Williams to strive for a classical sound, something with a melody viewers could relate to when thrust into the strange new galactic world he was creating.

Casting involved the same exhaustive process as it had for *American Graffiti*. Again George wanted to cast unknown actors in the lead roles, and again, the studio wanted bankable stars. George joined forces with director Brian De Palma, who was casting a horror movie called *Carrie*. After two months of seeing thirty to forty actors a day for five minutes at a time, George arrived at a trio of actors for the roles of Luke, Leia, and Han Solo. Jodie Foster and Amy Irving lost out to nineteen-year-old Carrie Fisher as Leia. Christopher Walken lost the role of Han Solo to Harrison Ford. Mark Hamill won the role of Luke, Lucas's namesake. Alec Guinness, a bankable name, didn't have to audition for the part of Obi-Wan Kenobi. The other featured actors were found in England.

In late 1975, Charles Lippincott, a former publicist at MGM, joined the *Star Wars* team as vice president of advertising, publicity, promotion, and merchandising. He'd seen the script and thought it would make a great comic book. Lippincott soon learned that George's plans were infinitely larger than just comic books. For three hours one day, George talked excitedly to Lippincott about opening two *Star Wars* stores. They would sell *Star Wars* comic books, R2-D2 mugs, C-3PO windup toys, and other film-related merchandise. George may have recognized the profit potential of merchandising (making and selling objects based on a film or book) as early as age eleven, when his family visited Disneyland. Walt Disney, one of George's heroes, was a master merchandiser, putting Mickey Mouse, Donald Duck, and other Disney characters in theme parks and on lunch boxes and toys.

Lippincott went to Marvel Comics and negotiated a publishing arrangement for *Star Wars* comic books. Meanwhile, George's attorney, Tom Pollock, struck a book deal with Ballantine, a leading science-fiction publishing house. Editor Judy-Lynn Del Rey planned to launch a new line of books at the end of 1976. The book deal meant that her new line would include a novelization of the *Star Wars* screenplay, a sequel, and a book about making the film.

Filming began in Tunisia in the spring of 1976. The desert there was a fine location for the main hero's home planet, Tatooine. George set a thirteen-week shooting schedule, but trouble dogged the filming from the beginning. The first exterior shot the script called for was a dry lake bed, which should be easy to find in a desert. But the day before filming began, rain fell in the Sahara Desert for the first time in fifty years. The lake bed was wet, and mud holes abounded.

Nor was all well with the two actors in the scene. Inside his golden C-3PO costume, Anthony Daniels was cut and bruised by the outfit's sharp plastic edges. He couldn't even sit down. Kenny Baker, who played the robot R2-D2, fared little better. Crammed into the costume with his elbows plastered to his sides, Baker

Star Wars *fans will be familiar with this dugout structure. In the movie, it was the set for Luke's house. It is really the home of a Tunisian family.*

could hardly operate the computer lights and radar eye on his face. His controls picked up Tunisian radio signals beautifully, however. Because of the noise inside his costume, Baker couldn't hear the director yell "Cut!" A crew member had to hit the shell with a hammer to stop Baker.

Finally George told Baker to get out of the costume. George tried to film the robot rolling along the desert by pulling the empty costume with a thin wire. It fell over. Then a fierce sandstorm battered the Jawa's huge sandcrawler, two stories high and ninety feet long. George lost a day rebuilding it, then shot the Jawa's scene the next day. He spent another day burning the wooden sandcrawler—a cheaper and easier method of getting rid of it than dismantling the huge set and taking it away.

Production moved to Elstree Studio near London for soundstage filming about two weeks later. Things continued to go wrong. Ben Kenobi, played by Alec Guinness, had nothing to do in the second half of the film, but the character was so important that he couldn't just be ignored. To explain Kenobi's absence, Marcia suggested they kill the character off. When Alec Guinness heard the plan, he threatened to quit. But George told him the truth—his role was crucial to the film's believability. After delicate negotiations, Guinness stayed.

On the bright side was the wardrobe by costume designer John Mollo. From Leia's medieval-looking robe to Han Solo's gunslinger look to the homespun sincerity of Luke's shirts, the costumes were terrific.

John Barry's sets were wrong, though. George told the crew to make everything look used. They groaned as they rolled R2-D2's shell in dirt, kicked it, and nicked its shiny paint with a saw.

No one could figure out what was going on in this oddball shoot, and George didn't bother to explain. Sometimes he didn't even bother to nod hello.

Some of the Star Wars *cast unmasked: Peter Mayhew,* upper left, *played Chewbaca; Kenny Baker,* lower left, *played R2-D2; Mark Hamill,* far right, *played Luke Skywalker; and Anthony Daniels,* second from right, *played C-3PO.*

George's relations with his British crew grew more and more strained. The studio had told the British director of photography to get rid of the gauzy, fairytale look George wanted. The cameraman listened to the studio without telling George. The cameraman should have been fired, but neither George nor Kurtz had it in him to do it.

The Americans did not understand British union rules either. British film crews quit at 5:30 P.M. sharp. George asked them to work longer in order to stay on schedule. Union workers had the right to vote on the issue. They did, and George lost. He countered by saving the easy shots for the end of the day. He also supervised simultaneous shoots by racing from one soundstage to another on a little bicycle.

Still the mishaps continued. Two weeks after Elstree production began, makeup supervisor Stuart Freeborn was hospitalized before he could finish the masks for the cantina scene. Actors could hardly breathe in their hurriedly completed masks until Kurtz picked up a razor blade and slit air holes in them. The remote-controlled version of R2-D2 walked into walls, and the overenthusiastic special-effects crew exploded entire sets. Some storm troopers were hurt in a scene, and one needed hospitalization. Marcia came to England, caught a severe case of flu, and also had to be hospitalized. When the background footage from ILM arrived, it looked so bad that George had to use an alternative method of filming that required hot lights on the sets. Unfortunately, England was also in the midst of a heat wave. Electricians fainted in the rafters, and Chewbacca collapsed.

Alan Ladd Jr., the Fox executive who had originally said yes to *Star Wars*, worried about the film's escalating costs. He flew to England and saw a rough cut, or unfinished version, of the film. Facing opposition from his studio's board of directors, Ladd cut off George's money supply. Ladd continued to believe in the film, calling it "possibly the greatest picture ever made," but he felt he had to resort to damage control.

If George had been running at full speed before, now he raced. He got Marcia to reedit the film. It looked a little better. He was sure he could fix it at home.

Except that at home, after a year of work and spending half their $2 million budget, Industrial Light & Magic had completed only three shots. George blew up; John Dykstra blew up right back. On his flight from L.A. to San Francisco that night, thirty-one-year-old George felt chest pains. They were worse by the time Marcia picked him up at the airport. They rushed to a hospital, where he was diagnosed with hypertension and exhaustion.

George left the hospital determined to regain control of the movie and supervise the special-effects photography. He pushed Dykstra into the background, but he used the computerized camera Dykstra had invented. The Dykstraflex camera moved—the model planes did not. Without the camera, the aerial dogfights between the X-wings and the TIE fighters couldn't have been done.

Some scenes had yet to be filmed—desert shots of R2-D2, the banthas, the land speeder. George made plans to shoot in the sizzling Death Valley desert in Southern California. The day before filming began there, George learned that Mark Hamill was in the hospital after a car crash. Thinking quickly, George eliminated Hamill's close-up shots, used a stand-in actor for long shots, and focused on getting the bantha on film. The bantha—played by an elephant unaccustomed to heat—kept shedding its steamy costume.

The film would have to come together in the editing. Since there was simply too much work for Marcia to do alone, George hired Richard Chew, then Paul Hirsch. George himself went from editing machine to editing machine, giving instructions. By January 1977, he had a first cut of the whole film.

By then, everyone, including George, was fed up with *Star Wars*. When director Martin Scorsese asked Marcia to edit his film *New York, New York* in Los

George works with one of the characters—Greedo. The actor is breathing through a straw poked into his stuffy mask.

Angeles, she took the job. Paul Hirsch finished up the *Star Wars* editing while George mixed the sound and sound effects. Carrie Fisher dropped by one day and found George lying exhausted on a couch. He looked at her and said hollowly, "I don't ever want to do this again."

But he was in too deep to quit. The friends he invited to screenings either criticized the film or expressed sympathy, which was worse. George resigned himself to failure. "I figured, well, it's just a silly movie. It ain't going to work," he said. Then he went to London to supervise the recording of John Williams's musical score and was encouraged to find that "it was the one thing on the picture that was better than I had ever imagined." His friend Carroll Ballard, who saw the film before and after the score was added, said the music made a mind-boggling difference.

Finally, all the pieces began to come together. The novelization of the screenplay had been published in November 1976 and was selling well. George's four years of *Star Wars* punishment came to an end on May 25, 1977, the day the film opened.

Early that day, George delivered the last reel of the film into the courier's hands. It arrived at one Los Angeles theater after the first reels had already begun to play.

Marcia and George leave the Academy Awards ceremony with an Oscar in hand.

Chapter **SEVEN**

THE YEAR'S BEST MOVIE

IT WAS **MAY 25, 1977. THE NEXT DAY, THE LUCASES** would fly to the island of Maui in Hawaii for a vacation, their first in years. Screenwriters Bill Huyck and Gloria Katz would join them there for ten days. Alan Ladd Jr. and his wife were also vacationing in Hawaii. The Lucases would meet up with the Ladds in Honolulu, and Steven Spielberg, who had become good friends with George, would join them. Both George and Spielberg liked to get out of town when their films opened to avoid the fuss.

The day before the trip, however, there was work to finish. George had been working nights to finish *Star Wars* in the editing room at the Samuel Goldwyn studio, while Marcia worked there during the day.

That evening, they ran into each other and decided to have dinner together. They headed for the Hamburger Hamlet on Hollywood Boulevard, near a famous movie theater called Mann's Chinese Theater.

In front of the theater, George said, it "was like a mob scene. One lane of traffic was blocked off. There were police there. There were limousines in front of the theater. There were lines, eight or nine people *wide*, going both ways and around the block." He thought, "'My God, what's going on here? It must be a premiere or something.' I looked at the marquee, and it was *Star Wars*." At the restaurant, he and Marcia sat by the window and stared out at the crowds.

Ted Mann, the new owner of what had been called Graumann's Chinese Theater, had agreed to run *Star Wars* for a month because the film he'd originally booked wasn't ready. If the booking was a fluke, the turnout wasn't. Gary Kurtz and Charles Lippincott had made sure of that. A 20th Century Fox publicity agent said, "The lines were there because Gary and Charlie went to a sci-fi convention every... weekend. Somehow Gary and Charlie translated the heart and the essence of the film. People asked, 'Well, how did the lines get there?' That's the only answer."

George went back to work that night feeling not so much exhilarated as stunned. It was a sheer stroke of luck that his film opened when it did, the Wednesday before Memorial Day weekend. This gave the film a great advantage, because people have more free time to spend in movie theaters on long holiday weekends. Instead of a typical three-day opening, *Star Wars* had six days.

When the Lucases flew to Hawaii the next day, they almost immediately began receiving phone calls from ecstatic Fox publicists. George had trouble taking in the news of the film's huge success. He was still winding down from the long strain of working eighteen-hour days for several weeks.

When Spielberg joined the group in Honolulu, legend has it that he and George went to the beach to build a sand castle. They also shared ideas for new projects. Spielberg said he wanted to make a James Bond type of film. George talked about an old idea he'd had about a playboy adventurer. Spielberg was enthusiastic.

So began their collaboration on the *Indiana Jones* films. It was decided that Spielberg would direct and George would be executive producer and cowriter. George was serious about never wanting to direct again.

Indiana Jones was named for the Lucases' black-and-white malamute dog, Indiana. It wasn't the first time the big dog had inspired a character. Because Indiana sat beside Marcia when she took him for a drive, George called him her furry copilot—like Chewbacca.

While the Lucases relaxed in Hawaii, *Star Wars* was making history back on the mainland. Viewers lined up at 8:00 A.M. to see the 10:00 A.M. show, and they kept lining up throughout the day. A headline in the show-business bible, the trade newspaper *Variety*, shrieked, "MAMMOTH 6 DAY DOMESTIC TAKE THE BEST SINCE JAWS." Ticket sales for the opening six days were reported at $2,556,418.

As more and more theaters began to show *Star Wars*, · the lines of students, sci-fi fans, businesspeople, and moms with kids kept growing, leaving piles of fast-food wrappers and soft-drink containers on the streets. In Los Angeles, 20th Century Fox sent teams to clean up the mess. Fox could afford to do some community service. After all, they had a real block-buster on their hands. Nightly news shows and national magazines ran features on the film's un-precedented and astonishing success. Some critics noted the film's weak story, but most responded to its fresh style and energy. The news weekly *Time* ran a six-page article titled *"Star Wars:* The Year's Best Movie."

Movie theater owners had to clear their theaters after each showing of *Star Wars.* If they didn't, viewers just kept sitting there. Albert Szabo, manager of the thousand-seat Avco Theater in Westwood, hired sixty extra staff members. The first week of June, he told the *Los Angeles Times*, "Last weekend we turned away five thousand people. This isn't a snowball, this is an avalanche."

The Lucases stayed in Hawaii for several weeks. They were content to miss the hoopla. Coming to grips with *Star Wars'* success was even harder for the more traditional Hollywood players. A week after the film opened, it was obvious that Hollywood's old rules no longer applied. Ladd suggested that the studio release John Williams's musical score for *Star Wars* as an album. But traditional wisdom held that orchestral scores didn't sell. But by the beginning of June 1977, two hundred thousand copies of the two-record album had sold. It eventually sold over a million copies in the United States alone.

In 1978, Fox released *Star Wars* internationally. George's merchandising dreams were also coming true. Back when George had negotiated the contract for *Star Wars,* he had asked Fox for the right to make a sequel and the right to keep profits from any merchandise based on the movie. Fox executives had been astonished. These rights meant nothing unless a film was a big hit. And they didn't expect *Star Wars* to be a smashing success. Fox sold the rights to make and sell toys to Kenner Toys—but George was allowed to keep some of the profits as well as control over the products.

George had always believed in his film. His company, Lucasfilm Ltd., had a merchandising department as big as Fox's. When the film was released, George told the *Los Angeles Times,* "In a way this film was designed around toys. I'm not making much for directing this movie. If I make money it will be from the toys." When the film became a phenomenal success, George said, "I didn't want someone using the name *Star Wars* on a piece of junk." He hired a manager to handle the new toy and product proposals that were

Ben Burtt collects his award for sound effects while Mark Hamill shares a special moment with costar C-3PO.

flooding in. To stop the bootleg market of *Star Wars* merchandise, George arranged to supply approved merchandise to the newly established *Star Wars* Official Fan Club.

George also began work on a sequel, *The Empire Strikes Back*. He had to make a sequel within two years or his right to do so would revert back to Fox, along with the rights to all future *Star Wars* pictures.

Star Wars was nominated for ten Oscars at the 1978 Academy Awards ceremony, including Best Picture and best director. It won six—for original score, editing, art direction, costume design, visual effects, and sound. Ben Burtt was also given a special sound achievement award.

George lost the Best Picture and Best Director awards to Woody Allen and *Annie Hall*. Although George had once said, "I'm an introvert. I don't want to be famous," fame had already brought unwanted rewards. Once, a knife-wielding fan walked into his office, claiming to be cowriter of *Star Wars,* and demanded his share of the profits. Another time, a group of fans claimed to have walked across the country "at God's behest" to find George.

By 1979, George's share of *Star Wars* profits was around $40 million, of which taxes took half. George again gave points to various people involved in the film's production. He also bought himself a gift. Still driving a 1969 Camaro, he bought a used Ferrari.

Most of the rest of the money went into tax-free municipal bonds, a safe investment. George planned to finance *The Empire Strikes Back* himself. In turn, he hoped, *Empire* would finance a project he had been thinking about for years. He had in mind a filmmaker community that would bring back to life the camaraderie and creativity of USC's Dirty Dozen. He planned to call the place Skywalker Ranch.

Billy Dee Williams played Lando Calrissian, a soldier of fortune turned respectable, in The Empire Strikes Back.

Chapter EIGHT

THE EMPIRE TAKES SHAPE

GEORGE SURVIVED BEING RICH AND FAMOUS THE SAME way he had survived being in debt—by working. But he changed his role to that of a creative mogul—a powerful behind-the-scenes force in Hollywood.

He saw himself and his friends as different from the moguls of Old Hollywood, the Samuel Goldwyns and Jack Warners, who had founded the big studios. George dismissed the current studio executives as corporate bureaucrats. Of his own circle, he said, "We are the pigs. We are the ones who sniff out the truffles. . . . who dig out the gold. . . . the power lies with us—the ones who actually know how to make movies."

After *Star Wars*, George's first business challenge was to negotiate a production deal for the sequel, *The*

Empire Strikes Back, that would allow him to retain the lion's share of the profits. His creative challenge was to find out if it was possible for him to work on a film as an executive producer. In this position, George would supply money and oversee the film's production, as well as provide creative input where needed. The day-to-day problems would be handled by an on-the-spot producer, the line producer. The director would deal with the actors.

George had written notes for a *Star Wars* sequel while working on the many drafts of the first film. In this episode, the rebels battle the Empire, and with Yoda's help, Luke comes close to understanding his heroic destiny. George gave his notes to screenwriter Leigh Brackett; sadly, she died of cancer only days after turning in her first draft. George knew the script had to sparkle. *Star Wars* fans would immediately spot any errors. Viewers wouldn't let dazzling special effects distract them from characters and story. But George didn't want to endure the agony of writing the script himself. Through Spielberg, he found Chicago advertising copywriter Lawrence Kasdan, with whom George could work on the inevitable changes and new drafts.

It was hard to find a director because directing *Empire* was a no-win proposition. If the sequel didn't match up to *Star Wars,* the director would be blamed. If it was just as good, the credit would go to George. Gary Kurtz, who would line-produce the film, talked to one of his old friends, Irvin Kerschner. Both were Zen

Buddhists; both liked Yoda. Kerschner said he would accept the challenge, and everybody breathed easier.

But on the first day of filming in March 1979, George surprised and shocked both Kurtz and Kerschner. "[George] came up to us and said, 'You know this is my own money and we have to be careful with it, so be sure you do a good job,'" Kurtz recalled. George's tactic did not inspire confidence!

Confrontation was par for the course for George during this time. Before beginning studio negotiations for *Empire,* he had fired his agent, saying he didn't need him anymore. His agent and the agency he worked for responded with a lawsuit that dragged on for years. In the end, the courts said the agent did not have the right to any of the profits from *Empire* or any other *Star Wars* sequel.

George also battled with producers of a TV show called *Battlestar Galactica,* which appeared on television soon after the success of *Star Wars.* George wrote a letter to *Variety* accusing the show of stealing his ideas and passing itself off as a "*Star Wars* for television." He called on Fox, the studio that had produced *Star Wars,* to keep *Battlestar* from airing. Fox filed a lawsuit to stop the show, but lost. The show became a hit.

Part of what was at issue in Fox's lawsuit was that John Dykstra had contributed to the special effects for *Battlestar.* ILM had been founded to develop the technology needed to film *Star Wars,* and Dykstra's computerized Dykstraflex camera had done that. But when George moved ILM to San Rafael in late 1978, he had not asked Dykstra to come along. He hadn't given Dykstra any points in *Star Wars* profits, either. Their argument still bothered both men.

Dykstra stayed in the special-effects business, working out of ILM's Van Nuys warehouse. His first and badly needed clients were the producers of *Battlestar.* Even though Dykstra had developed his special-effects technology while working for George, he still owned the right to use that technology. It may not have been ethically right for him to use the technology for another company, but his actions were legally acceptable. Fox's lawsuit against *Battlestar* dragged on for years, until a judge finally ruled against Fox.

In spite of all the conflict, George continued to work as executive producer on two films, *The Empire Strikes Back* and another sequel, *More American Graffiti.* He kept nudging Kurtz to hurry Kerschner on *Empire,* but that wasn't easy to achieve. Kerschner, Kurtz, cast member Mark Hamill, and about seventy crew members were working in hideous conditions in Norway to film the planet Hoth sequences. They had begun filming on March 5, 1979, at the end of the worst winter northern Europe had seen in years. The *Empire* group endured blizzards, whiteouts, an avalanche, and average temperatures of minus ten degrees, without taking windchill into account.

Production on the Dagobah sequences began at Elstree Studios in England a week after the Hoth

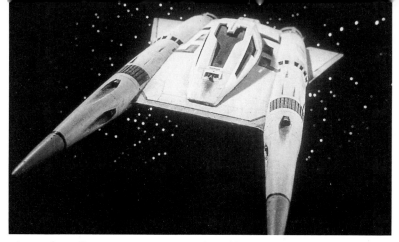

The Dykstraflex camera was used to film some of the star-ship scenes in Battlestar Gallactica. *Although the ships looked like they were moving, it was the computerized camera that moved.*

crew left for Norway. George came to Elstree for two weeks to launch the British portion of the filming. He'd done everything he could to prepare for the shoot, down to storyboarding every scene.

But as usual, nothing ran smoothly. When Kerschner, Kurtz, Hamill, and crew arrived in England from Norway, they found multiple problems. A fire had totaled one whole stage. Noxious gases had filled the bog planet set. On June 6, 1979, second-unit director John Barry had an afternoon headache that led to his death by 2:00 A.M. of infectious meningitis. Time and money were in short supply.

After George returned to the United States, he phoned Kurtz every day, urging him to speed up. When that didn't work, he stormed over. Furious after seeing a rough cut, he turned on Kurtz, Kerschner, and editor Paul Hirsch and accused them of sabotage, of purposely ruining his movie. Then George locked himself in the editing suite for two days, emerging with a reedited version of the film. When the others objected to its choppiness, George became angry and declared, "I'm on the hook for the money."

In fact, George's money was running out. He had to ask 20th Century Fox to underwrite some loans. Fox agreed to put up more money. In exchange, they took back some of the profits George had won earlier in negotiations. George blamed Kurtz.

On August 31, 1979, cast and crew members celebrated the end of filming *Empire* at a wrap party. Plans for a third film were already under way. The new film, then called *Revenge of the Jedi,* continued the conflict between the rebels and the Empire. In this episode, the secret of Luke and Darth Vader's relationship is revealed and peace is restored. Kurtz wouldn't be working on *Jedi,* however. Another Lucasfilm casualty was publicist Charlie Lippincott, who left the company's growing bureaucracy. The originally lean staff had ballooned in size to fill lavish offices near Universal Studios.

Empire opened on May 21, 1980. Fans camped outside theaters for days before the opening. "We are waiting for our high," said Terri Hardi, a fan who had seen *Star Wars* 178 times. Film critics were generous. Even *New Yorker* critic Pauline Kael, who had panned George's earlier films, was won over by the slower paced, more intellectual *Empire.*

But people in the movie industry were not pleased with one thing they saw on the screen—the film's credits. Soon after *Empire* opened, the Director's

Guild of America (DGA) fined George $250,000 for not showing director Irvin Kershner's credit at the beginning of the film. George protested that his style was to run the credits at the end, but the DGA insisted. George and the DGA came to a private settlement. Next, the Writers Guild fined him $15,000 for not giving Kasdan adequate credit. Fed up, George abruptly slashed his ties with Hollywood. He resigned from the Director's and Writers guilds and from the Academy of Motion Picture Arts and Sciences, and he moved all Lucasfilm offices from Los Angeles to San Rafael, next to ILM.

Lucasfilm's ILM division began work on its first non-Lucasfilm picture in 1980. That same year, the Lucasfilm computer division was formed to work on digital imagery and audio postproduction. In October, *Fortune* magazine ran a feature about George, who had built a personal fortune of $100 million in just three years. His company employed nearly two hundred people and earned $1.5 million a week. In a photo, a proud George watched bulldozers prepare the land on Bull Pit Ranch in Marin County for construction of his long-anticipated Skywalker Ranch.

A highly successful businessman, George was also an intensely private person. His switch from filmmaker to producer made it easier for him to protect his private life. He preferred to operate behind the scenes instead of in the spotlight. Still, film remained his obsession, requiring the same intense effort and energy that had marked his earlier, more public life. He was incapable of leaving his work at the office. He told friends that his behavior was hard on Marcia, putting a strain on their marriage.

In 1981, one of the highlights of George's life was the release of *Raiders of the Lost Ark,* a joint project with director Steven Spielberg. It was an enormously popular film, although some critics thought the film's violence was inappropriate for young viewers. The film received Oscars for art direction, sound, film editing, and visual effects, as well as a special award for sound-effects editing.

That year, too, George found a director for *Return of the Jedi*—Richard Marquand. Howard Kazanjian would be line producer. Lawrence Kasdan's script would again be based on George's story. From July to December 1981, Marquand, Kazanjian, and Kasdan constructed the storyboards. In addition, that year George worked as the uncredited executive producer on Kasdan's directorial debut, *Body Heat.* George hoped critics would be kinder when reviewing the movie if his name wasn't associated with it. This was the first of many times George served as an "insurance policy" for his friends. If they ran into trouble with a film, he was there to help.

In many ways, the year 1982 was business as usual for George. Production on *Jedi* began in London in January. George remained there for the entire shoot. One-third of the film's $30 million budget had been earmarked for the design of various creatures, but only sixty of the hundreds that were developed made it into the film. The teddy-bearlike Ewoks did.

To aid in *Jedi* postproduction, Lucasfilm introduced the THX Sound System, a service dedicated to improving the quality of film sound and image in public and home theaters. A related service, the Theatre Alignment Program, was also initiated. This program checked release prints of films and aligned theater projection and sound equipment.

That year, George also served as executive producer for his friend John Korty's animated film, *Twice Upon a Time*. Lucas found his life as a producer satisfying. As one of the richest people in America, George had money to invest in his friends' projects, but he didn't have to deal with the day-to-day struggles of being a director or line producer.

Some events of 1982 were not business as usual, however. Early that year, George and Marcia adopted two-year-old Amanda. George was eager to spend time with her. "You can't put a kid on hold and say, 'Wait, I've got one more picture to do, you just sit tight,'" he said. "You know she's only going to be two once, and she's great and I'm not going to miss it."

Return of the Jedi was released on May 25, 1983. It was a box-office smash, grossing $45 million by the end of the first week. Five books based on *Jedi* made the June 11 *New York Times* bestseller list, and the film later won a special Oscar for visual effects.

Not everyone loved the film. Pauline Kael criticized the whole *Star Wars* enterprise, saying that the Ewoks were obviously contrived just to sell merchandise. And in fact, forty pages of the Kenner toy catalog were devoted to cuddly Ewok items. Other film critics were jaded by the repetition of the *Star Wars* formula. *Newsweek's* David Ansen wrote, "The innocence that made *Star Wars* the movie phenomenon of the 1970s has long since vanished. It has become its own relentless Empire, grinding out Fun with soulless efficiency."

A week or so after the May 25 opening of *Jedi*, the Lucases announced the end of their marriage. They did not reveal any details about their divorce, other than the obvious fact that it was hurtful and costly. Amanda stayed with George. Tabloid newspapers made much of his subsequent relationship with singer Linda Ronstadt.

After the divorce, George poured his energy into work. For the next several years, Lucasfilm bustled with projects, from the successful *Indiana Jones* sequels to the unsuccessful *Howard the Duck*. There were television spin-offs—about Ewoks, droids, and a young Indiana Jones—and there were games—large-scale ones like *Star Tours* for Disneyland and Walt Disney World as well as home computer games. One of the games inspired the television series *Maniac Mansion*. Lucasfilm's computer division, Pixar, was sold to Apple Computer founder Steven Jobs in 1986. There was even a go at developing a cyberspace community, though it was dropped when it did not prove lucrative.

Lucasfilm's achievements were driven by the growth in computer technology and its widening acceptance in society. After all, you can't play in cyberspace unless you have a personal computer and access to the Internet. A prime example of Lucasfilm's use of technology is the television series *Young Indiana Jones Chronicles,* which first aired on March 4, 1992, on ABC. The idea behind the series was that a young Indiana Jones, or Young Indy, would walk through twentieth-century history, learning and experiencing all sorts of things, from the history of jazz to social conditions during different times. Through computer technology, Young Indy seemed to be part of historical events.

ABC had agreed to broadcast thirty-two hours of the show, but the network canceled the series after twenty-eight hours. Some of the shows were never seen. Lucasfilm developed a new strategy. All the shows were reedited and expanded into twenty-two feature-length films in videotape format. When the technology of digital video discs (DVD) becomes widely accepted, the movies will be further expanded into interactive, multimedia experiences.

What makes all this possible is a production technique George calls "nonlinear filmmaking." Traditional filmmaking involves three basic stages: preproduction, production, and postproduction. Nonlinear film-making is technology based. George has a film crew in the studio at all times, and the content of what they film can change as the shows or films develop. Scripts have always been rewritten, but George believes the shows themselves can be rewritten almost instantaneously.

As an executive producer, George has finally achieved his ideal work situation—other people write the script and get the footage, then they turn it over to him to shape and edit. Changes are no longer made with the old, laborious Moviola process, cutting and splicing celluloid strips of film. Using a digital camera instead of a film camera, images can be sent electronically anywhere in the world and edited on computer. There's no longer any need to touch film to edit it. A director can edit a scene and reshoot it the next day from the comfort of his or her electronic study, without ever going to the filming location or interacting with actors. George is doing just that.

The ease and speed of this kind of filming gives George time to devote to new passions. In 1991, he established the nonprofit George Lucas Educational Foundation. According to its mission statement, the foundation grew from George's belief that "education is the most important investment we can make to secure the future of our democracy." The foundation seeks to improve public schools by integrating new technology into the current educational system.

George's high school teachers probably never would have dreamed that their lackluster student would one day put so much energy and money into education. His high school classmates even decided to erect a sculpture in George Lucas Plaza in Modesto in honor of the car-crazy teen they knew. The sculpture is of a teenage boy and girl and a '57 Chevy.

Other old wounds were salved when the Academy of Motion Picture Arts and Sciences Board of Governors gave George the Irving Thalberg Award for being a "creative producer whose body of work reflects a consistently high quality of motion picture production." He didn't rejoin the Academy, but he accepted the award. In his March 30, 1992, acceptance speech, George made his new priority clear: "All of us who make motion pictures are teachers; teachers with very loud voices."

There are many ways to teach. One is by being a role model. On that basis, George was inducted into the Academy of Achievement in 1989. He appears in

This statue, commemorating the sentiments depicted in American Graffiti, *stands in George Lucas Plaza in Modesto, California.*

George and two of his daughters, Amanda, left, *and Katie, take a ride through Disney World.*

the Hall of Business, along with leaders such as Oprah Winfrey and Martha Stewart, individuals who "shaped the twentieth century by their accomplishments." When the achievement academy asked George who was especially important to him as a kid, he mentioned his parents and "a high school English teacher who was just brilliant." He even remembered that teacher's name—Mr. Fagan. George went on, "I don't know whether he taught me very much, but he certainly inspired me to be creative and try to write things. And when you think about your best teachers, they are people that you look up to and are inspired by more than people who actually got the concepts across to you."

George has the opportunity to be an even more direct role model for his own children. In addition to Amanda, he adopted another daughter, Katie, in 1987 and later a son, Jett. He is a single parent.

By 1985, George had bought 4,750 acres of land in Marin County. In October 1996, Marin County's Board of Supervisors voted to approve George's proposal for construction of an $87 million digital film and interactive multimedia compound. By December, newspapers reported that the Save Our Countywide Plan Committee had filed a lawsuit to stop George. The committee wanted to keep Marin County's rural character.

George bought even more land—and he did so in an underhanded way, by using his accountant's name. When the news leaked out, many people in the county were outraged.

George has said that the "object is to try and make the system work for you, instead of against you. And the only way you can do that is through success, I'm afraid." It appears that he was once again successful. He came to an agreement with Marin County to tuck the new complex into the rolling hills, unseen from the highway but adjoining the buildings of Skywalker Ranch. In late 1998, construction had not yet begun.

The Ranch, sometimes referred to as Lucasland, is corporate headquarters for George's five companies. Approximately seventeen hundred employees enjoy a softball diamond with a 150-player league and a fitness center equipped with weight and aerobic rooms, racquetball and basketball courts, and a twenty-five-meter pool. Work schedules are flexible, and there is no dress code.

George relaxes at his expansive corporate office—Skywalker Ranch.

Chapter **NINE**

MEANWHILE, BACK AT THE RANCH

THE CENTERPIECE OF SKYWALKER RANCH, THE MAIN
House, stands beside a quiet lake. Built in the Victorian
style, the Main House holds George's offices and
Lucasfilm's extensive library. George designed the building himself. The sun-filled atrium is climate controlled.
Staffers can eat lunch on benches around the central
garden. The Main House also features a winding stair-
case, antiques, original paintings by Maxfield Parrish
and Norman Rockwell, Tiffany chandeliers, and
stained-glass windows. A time capsule filled with *Star
Wars* artifacts is buried in a corner of the building.

The Technical Building was designed to look like an
old brick winery. And, in fact, it is next to a vineyard
of several acres. Directors, producers, editors, and

Scenes in Episode I were filmed in the theater of this Italian palace.

writers who come to work at the Ranch can stay at
the Inn, which resembles a New England farmhouse
from the late 1800s. The Greenhouse is part of the
Organic Garden, and much of the harvest is used in
the Ranch's kitchens.

George's corporate headquarters may be state-of-the-
art, but, he says, his personal life isn't. "I interact with
a couple of hundred people every single day, and it's
very intense. I've got three kids, so I interact with
them whatever's left of the day. The few brief seconds
I have before I fall asleep are usually more meditative
in nature."

Since 1994, when George invited a *Variety* reporter
to the Ranch to break the news that he would direct
again, he has been working on the "prequels" to *Star
Wars*. The first is called *Star Wars:* Episode I *The
Phantom Menace*. Secrecy surrounded its filming.

In a 1990 interview with film critic Roger Ebert,

George mapped out the contents of Episodes I, II, and III. The new *Star Wars* episodes deal with young Obi-Wan Kenobi and Anakin Skywalker before he became Darth Vader. In this episode, Anakin Skywalker (also Luke and Leia's father) is only nine years old. George told Ebert, "The number three film is the one that Luke gets born in, so there's about a twenty-year stretch between [episodes] three and four [the fourth being *Star Wars,* in which Luke Skywalker is about twenty years old]. I would say that those three [the *Star Wars* trilogy] happen in about ten years or something. Maybe not quite that long."

Filming on Episode I began in July 1997 at the Royal Palace in Caserta, Italy. At a press conference, Lucas explained the plot in vague terms: "There is a queen in a society in the film who is a pivotal character."

The young queen is played by Natalie Portman. Liam Neeson stars as an esteemed Jedi Knight and Ewan McGregor as the young Obi-Wan Kenobi. Ian McDiarmid is back as Palpatine, still the bad guy. Yoda's back, too, and California child actor Jake Lloyd has been cast as Anakin Skywalker. The film was released in May 1999.

With this new film, George was taking yet another gamble. The world had changed since 1977, when personal computers didn't exist. His private world had also changed. The responsibilities of children, a large network of companies, and his educational foundation keep him from getting lost in filmmaking.

Natalie Portman plays a very important queen in Episode I.

Whatever the success of Episode I, there's no doubt that George has changed the film industry by uniting entertainment, business, and technology. He's made respectable pursuits of special effects and merchandising. He has made the Memorial Day weekend one of the most popular film release dates—it's called George Lucas Weekend by some people in Hollywood. And unlike most other Hollywood moguls, he has plowed his profits back into the industry, as well as applying his unique slant to public education.

A complicated, intriguing, and intelligent person, George is also humble. He knows his films aren't brain surgery or rocket science. They are exactly what he started out to make—movies a ten-year-old boy would love. They have given him creative independence and wealth. George Lucas himself has said that he thinks his films are kind of dumb. But the bottom line is, millions of fans disagree.

SOURCES

8   Dale Pollock, *Skywalking: The Life and Films of George Lucas* (New York:, Harmony Books, 1983), 24.

11   Charles Champlin, *George Lucas: The Creative Impulse: Lucasfilm's First Twenty-Five Years,* rev. ed. (New York: Abrams, 1997), 16.

13   Pollock, *Skywalking,* 15.

13   Ibid, 19.

16   Ibid.

16   Ibid.

16   Ibid., 22.

16   "George Lucas Interview," *Academy of Achievement,* June 2, 1995, <http://www.achievement.org/autodoc/page/luc0int-1> (8/14/98).

17   Pollock, *Skywalking,* 24.

18   Ibid., 27.

18   Ibid., 39.

19   Ibid., 38.

21   Pollock, *Skywalking,* 43.

22   Michael Pye and Lynda Myles, *The Movie Brats: How the Film Generation Took Over Hollywood* (New York: Holt, Rinehart and Winston, 1979), 115.

23   Champlin, *The Creative Impulse,* 18.

24   Garry Jenkins, *Empire Building: The Remarkable Real Life Story of Star Wars* (Secaucus, NJ: Citadel Press, 1997), 11.

25   Ibid., 11–12.

29   Pollock, *Skywalking,* 62.

30   Ibid., 69.

30   Jenkins, *Empire Building,* 14.

30   Pollock, *Skywalking,* 59.

30   Ibid., 39.

32   Ibid., 70.

33   Pye and Myles, *The Movie Brats,* 9.
36   Ibid., 68.
36   Pollock, *Skywalking,* 72.
36   Champlin, *The Creative Impulse,* 7.
37   Pollock, *Skywalking,* 76.
38   Ibid., 83.
39   Champlin, *The Creative Impulse,* 19.
39   Pollock, *Skywalking,* 79.
40   Champlin, *The Creative Impulse,* 23.
41   Pollock, *Skywalking,* 79.
43   Pye and Myles, *The Movie Brats,* 132.
43–44 Ibid., 118.
44   Pollock, *Skywalking,* 94.
45   Ibid.
46   Ibid., 92.
46   Ibid., 163.
47   Ibid., 96.
49   Ibid.
49   Ibid., 92.
53   Ibid., 27.
56   Ibid., 24.
57–58 Champlin, *The Creative Impulse,* 32.
59   Pollock, *Skywalking,* 92.
61   Pye and Myles, *The Movie Brats,* 126.
62   Pollock, *Skywalking,* 119.
62   Ibid.
62   Ibid.
63   Champlin, *The Creative Impulse,* 35.
63–64 Pauline Kael, *Reeling* (New York: Warner
         Books, 1976), 268.
64   Pollock, *Skywalking,* 106.
65   Champlin, *The Creative Impulse,* 35.
66   Ibid., 26.
67   Ibid., 57.
69   Pye and Myles, *The Movie Brats,* 132–133.
70   Champlin, *The Creative Impulse,* 42.

70 Pye and Myles, *The Movie Brats,* 134.
71 Pollock, *Skywalking,* 134.
71 Jenkins, *Empire Building,* 40.
72 Pollock, *Skywalking,* 139.
73 Champlin, *The Creative Impulse,* 45.
76 Pollock, *Skywalking,* 178.
76 Champlin, *The Creative Impulse,* 45.
83 Pollock, *Skywalking,* 175.
85 Champlin, *The Creative Impulse,* 55.
85 Pollock, *Skywalking,* 180.
85 Ibid., 181.
88 Champlin, *The Creative Impulse,* 55.
88 Jenkins, *Empire Building,* 159.
90 Ibid., 162–163.
90 Ibid., 163.
91 Ibid., 171.
91 Pollock, *Skywalking,* 193.
92 Mason Wiley and Damien Bona, *Inside Oscar: The Unofficial History of the Academy Awards* (New York: Ballantine, 1986), 538.
95 Pye and Myles, *The Movie Brats,* 9.
97 Jenkins, *Empire Building,* 202.
97 Pollock, *Skywalking,* 189.
100 Jenkins, *Empire Building,* 211–212.
100 Ibid., 225.
103 Ibid., 251.
104 Ibid., 195.
105 Champlin, *The Creative Impulse,* 160.
106 "The George Lucas Educational Foundation: A Storyteller for Education," *George Lucas Educational Foundation,* n.d., <http://www.glef.org/foundation> (7/14/98).
107 "Company History," *Lucasfilm Ltd. website,* n.d., <http://www.lucasfilm.com/history.html> (5/11/98).

107 Eric Barker, "George Lucas," *Jones Telecommunications and Multimedia Encyclopedia,* n.d., <http://www.digitalcentury.com/encyclo/update/lucas.html> (6/4/98).

108 "Gallery of Achievers," *Academy of Achievement,* n.d., <http://www.achievement.org/autodoc/pagegen/galleryachieve.html> (8/14/98).

108 "George Lucas Interview."

109 Pollock, *Skywalking,* 198.

112 Kevin Kelly and Paula Parisi, "Beyond Star Wars: What's Next For George Lucas," *Wired 5.02,* February, 1997, <http://www.wired.com/5.02/features/fflcas.html> (6/4/98).

113 Ebert and Siskel, *The Future of the Movies,* 95.

113 Joal Ryan, "Cameras Roll on 'Star Wars' Prequel," *E! Online News,* n.d., <http://eonline.com/News/Items/0,1,1552,00.html> (6/4/98).

SELECTED BIBLIOGRAPHY

BOOKS

Bouzereau, Laurent. *Star Wars: The Annotated Screenplays.* New York: Ballantine Books, 1997.

Champlin, Charles. *George Lucas: The Creative Impulse: Lucasfilm's First Twenty-Five Years,* rev. ed. New York: Abrams, 1997.

Dmytryk, Edward. *On Film Editing.* Boston: Focal Press, 1984.

Ebert, Roger, and Gene Siskel. *The Future of the Movies.* Kansas City: Andrews and McNeel, 1991.

Henderson, Mary. *Star Wars: The Magic of Myth.* New York: Bantam, 1997.

Jenkins, Garry. *Empire Building: The Remarkable Real Life Story of Star Wars.* Secaucus, NJ: Citadel Press, 1997.

Kael, Pauline. *Reeling.* New York: Warner Books, 1976.

Legrand, Catherine. *Chronicle of the Cinema.* New York: Dorling Kindersley, 1995.

Mast, Gerald. *A Short History of the Movies,* 4th ed. New York: Macmillan, 1986.

Murch, Walter. *In the Blink of an Eye: A Perspective on Film Editing.* Los Angeles: Silman-James Press, 1995.

Nicholls, Peter. *The World of Fantastic Films: An Illustrated Survey.* New York: Dodd, Mead & Company, 1984.

Wiley, Mason, and Damien Bona. *Inside Oscar: The Unofficial History of the Academy Awards.* New York: Ballantine, 1986.

ARTICLES

Barker, Eric. "George Lucas." *Jones Telecommunications and Multimedia Encyclopedia.* <http://www.digitalcentury.com/encyclo/update/lucas.html> (6/4/98).

Farmer, F. Randall. "Social Dimensions of Habitat's Citizenry." <http://www.communities.com/company/papers/citizenry.html> (7/14/98).

"Former classmates honor Lucas." October 5, 1995. <http://canoe2.canoe.ca/JamMoviesArtistsL/lucas_george.html> (6/4/98).

"George Lucas." *Celebsite*. <http://www.celebsite.com/people/georgelucas> (6/4/98).

"George Lucas Interview." *Academy of Achievement*, June 2, 1995. <http://www.achievement.org/autodoc/page/luc0int-1> (8/14/98).

Hale, Lynne. "Making Episode One: Lynne's Dary, Introduction & All I Need Is an Idea." <http://www.starwars.com/making/01/ides.html> (8/11/98).

Holeman, Heidi. "George Lucas' Empire strikes back forcefully." *The Oklahoma Daily*, February 21, 1997. <http://www.daily.on.edu/issues/spring1997/feb-21/empire.html> (6/4/98).

Kelly, Kevin, and Paula Parisi. "Beyond Star Wars: What's Next for George Lucas." *Wired 5.02*, February, 1997. <http://www.wired.com/wired/5.02/features/fflucas.html> (6/4/98).

"Lucas expands empire." October 30, 1996. <http://canoe2.canoe.ca/JamMoviesArtistsL/lucas_george.html> (6/4/98).

Lucas, George, and Senator Bob Kerrey, "Access to Education." *Wired 2.09*, September, 1994. <http://ig.cs.tuberlin.de/PE/WIRED/2.09/departments/idees.fortes/access.ed.html> (6/16/98).

Mattingly, Terry. "George Lucas, the Force and God." January 29, 1997. <http://www1.gospelcom.net/tmattingly/col.01.29.97.html> (6/4/98).

Parisi, Paula. "The Teacher Who Designs Videogames." *Wired 5.01*, January, 1997. <http://www.wired.com/wired/5.01/esschilling.html> (5/11/98).

Ryan, Joal. "Cameras Roll on 'Star Wars' Prequel." *E! Online News*. <http://eonline.com/News/Items/0,1,1552,00.html> (6/4/98).

PERSONAL COMMUNICATION

Cole, Jeanne. Lucasfilm Marketing Project Manager. Correspondence with author. August 25, 1998.

Scofield, Danielle. LucasLearning. Voice mail to author. June 3, 1998.

FILMOGRAPHY

PRODUCER FILMOGRAPHY

Indiana Jones and the Lost Continent (2001)
Star Wars: Episode I (1999)
Radioland Murders (1994)
The Young Indiana Jones Chronicles (1992) (TV)
Wow! (1990) (TV)
Indiana Jones and the Last Crusade (1989)
Willow (1988)
Tucker: The Man and His Dream (1988)
The Land Before Time (1988)
Star Tours (1987)
Labyrinth (1986)
Howard the Duck (1986)
Captain Eo
Droids (1985) (TV)
Ewoks (1985) (TV)
Ewoks: The Battle for Endor (1985) (TV)
Indiana Jones and the Temple of Doom (1984)
The Ewok Adventure (1984) (TV)
Return of the Jedi (1983)
Twice Upon a Time (1983)
Raiders of the Lost Ark (1981)
Body Heat (1981)
Kagemusha (1980)
The Empire Strikes Back (1980)
Star Wars (1977)
The Rain People (1969, associate producer)

WRITER FILMOGRAPHY

Star Wars: Episode III (2005) Story
Star Wars: Episode II (2002) Story
Star Wars: Episode I (1999)
Radioland Murders (1994) Story
Indiana Jones and the Last Crusade (1989) Story
Willow (1988) Story
Ewoks: The Battle for Endor (1985) (TV) Story
Indiana Jones and the Temple of Doom (1984) Story
The Ewok Adventure (1984) (TV) Story
Return of the Jedi (1983) Story
Raiders of the Lost Ark (1981) Story
The Empire Strikes Back (1980) Story
More American Graffiti (1979)
Star Wars (1977)
American Graffiti (1973)
THX 1138 (1970) Also earlier screenplay
Filmmaker (1968)
Anyone Lived in a Pretty How Town (1967)
THX 1138:4EB (1967)
1:42:08 A Man and His Car (1966)
Freiheit (1966)

Herbie (1966)
Look at Life (1965)

DIRECTOR FILMOGRAPHY

Star Wars: Episode I (1999)
Star Wars (1977)
American Graffiti (1973)
THX 1138 (1970)
Filmmaker (1968)
6.18.67 (1967)
*Anyone Lived in a Pretty How
    Town* (1967)
The Emperor (1967)
THX 1138:4EB (1967)
Freiheit (1966)
Herbie (1966)
Look at Life (1965)

EDITOR FILMOGRAPHY

Jurassic Park (1993)
    (uncredited)
THX 1138 (1970)
Filmmaker (1968)
6-18-67 (1967)
*Anyone Lived in a Pretty How
    Town* (1967)
1:42:08 (1966)
Herbie (1966)
Freiheit (1965)
Look at Life (1965)

CINEMATOGRAPHER FILMOGRAPHY

Gimme Shelter (1970)
Filmmaker (1968)
6.18.67 (1967)
*Anyone Lived in a Pretty How
    Town* (1967)
1:42:08 (1966)
Freiheit (1966)
Herbie (1966)
Look at Life (1965)

ACTOR FILMOGRAPHY

Beverly Hills Cop III (1994)
    Disappointed Man
*The Magical World of Chuck
    Jones* (1992)
*Hearts of Darkness: A
    Filmmaker's Apocalypse*
    (1991)
Star Tours (1987)
    Supervisor at Spaceport

MISCELLANEOUS CREW FILMOGRAPHY

Return to Oz (1985)
    (special thanks)
Filmmaker (1968) (sound)

INDEX

OTHER TITLES IN LERNER'S BIOGRAPHY® SERIES:

Arthur Ashe
Christopher Reeve
Jesse Owens
Legends of Dracula
Louisa May Alcott
Madeleine Albright

Maya Angelou
Mother Teresa
Nelson Mandela
Princess Diana
Rosie O'Donnell
Women in Space

ABOUT THE AUTHOR

Dana White has written a lot about the arts, including articles, columns, and seventeen books for young readers—several of them ALA Notables. A critic of juvenile literature for nearly twenty years, Ms. White is intrigued by why changes in the arts happen and how they impact society. The emphasis on world culture in George Lucas's *Star Wars* films was also a powerful "force" in shaping her interest in the man who made these groundbreaking films.

PHOTO ACKNOWLEDGMENTS

AP/Wide World Photos, 2, 86, 92, 112; © Modesto Bee, 6, 12; courtesy of Modesto Convention and Visitors Bureau, 10, 107; Hollywood Book and Poster, 14; Seth Poppel Yearbook Archives, 17; UPI/Corbis-Bettmann, 20, 34, 54; USC Moving Image Archive, 24; Don Hogan Charles/New York Times Co./Archive Photos, 26; Frank Edwards/Fotos International/Archive Photos, 29, 40; Archive Photos, 43; © Phil Loftus/London Features International (USA) Ltd., 48; Globe Photos, Inc., 50; Lou Lamb Smith, 57; © Photofest, 65, 72, 82, 99; © Hollywood Archive/London Features International (USA) Ltd., 68; © Ronald Siemoneit/SYGMA, 77; © János Kalmár, 80; © Richard Chambury/Alpha/Globe Photos, Inc., 81; © Ron Wolfson/London Features International (USA) Ltd., 94; © Pascal Della Zuaha/SYGMA, 108; © Jim Wilson/ New York Times Co./Archive Photos, 110; © Gregg DeGuire/London Features International (USA) Ltd., 114.

Cover photos
Hardcover: front, © Lisa Rose/Globe Photos, Inc.; back © Agence France Presse/Corbis-Bettmann.
Softcover: front, Pancha/Corbis; back, Agence France Presse/Corbis-Bettmann.